# THE SIEGE OF RABAUL

## By

## Henry Sakaida

**PHALANX**
Publishing Co., Ltd.
1051 Marie Avenue
St. Paul, MN 55118 U.S.A.
612/454-0607

ISBN: 1-883809-09-6

Library of Congress Card No. 95-72892

Text by Henry Sakaida

Cover Design by John Valo

Published by:
Phalanx Publishing Co., Ltd.
1051 Marie Ave. W.
St. Paul, MN 55118-4131 USA

European Distribution by:
Air Research Publications
P.O. Box 223, Walton on Thames
Surrey, KT12 3YQ
Great Britain

Printed in the United States of America

# INTRODUCTION

Nowadays, about 50 years have passed since the end of the Pacific War. I still think about Rabaul once in a while. What I remember is not that of the difficult times and sad events, but of the superb landscape of the bay, the volcanoes, the brilliance of the Southern Cross, and so on.

I think it is natural that people, especially the young, do not know about Rabaul or have even heard of its name. Now, through this book, they will come to understand what Rabaul was about.

I am indeed very pleased that writer Henry Sakaida has chosen to tell the story of Rabaul's Last Eagles. As the executive officer of Rabaul's last Zero fighter squadron in 1944-45, I remember the constant death and destruction by Allied Air Forces, the hardships of surviving in the tropical jungle environment, and the gallantry of our men under those trying circumstances. The full story can never be told, but Mr. Sakaida has worked hard to try and save as much as possible for the sake of both of our nations' histories.

The Allied veterans of the Rabaul Campaign will find our story fascinating. Although we wore different uniforms, we all had many things in common. We were all young men once, torn away from our families, filled with patriotic pride, and thrust into battle in the tropical Southeast Pacific. We all lost close friends and comrades and we still share this sense of loss.

I'm grateful to our nameless mechanics, engineers, and groundcrews who kept our aircraft flying. Our pilots not only fought against overwhelming odds, but also took tremendous risks on their long range reconnaissance missions to the Admiralty Islands. The crews from our sister squadron, the 958th Seaplane Unit, flew dangerous night missions against American PT boats and delivered scarce medical supplies to our troops on Bougainville Island.

Although Rabaul was bypassed by Allied Forces and we operated with only a handful of old aircraft, Admiral Jin-Ichi Kusaka, his staff, and enlisted men demonstrated their fighting spirit by successfully attacking targets in the Admiralties, long after our opponents had written us off. In spirit and mind, we were never defeated!

The guns of war at Rabaul have been silent for almost half a century and our two great nations are at peace; there is goodwill and friendship. Let us look back now so that we may never have to repeat this tragic history as we strive forward.

Tomoyoshi Hori
Former Commander
Japanese Imperial Navy

Hofu City
Yamaguchi Prefecture
September 21, 1994

# PREFACE

Scenario: Southeast Pacific, 1944. A group of ragtag fighter pilots, mostly sick and inexperienced, are abandoned to their fate on an inhospitable jungle island. They are left with a handful of broken down aircraft against overwhelming odds. They are expected to do the impossible – to defend their forces. Their commander goes one step further – he strikes back. Sounds like a plot for a Hollywood action movie?

Fact is indeed stranger than fiction. How many times have we watched a war flick on television or at the movies, and thought, "What a tired story. I already know the plot."

Filled with clichés and improbable situation, we shake our heads in disbelief. But World War II was indeed filled with clichés and improbable situations and much more.

History seems to have bypassed the Rabaul Campaign after February 1944 as our forces rushed toward the Philippines and Japan. A small but determined band of Japanese rebuilt their squadron from the scrap heap and fought back. They staged a mini Pearl Harbor type attack in the Admiralty Islands – twice. They literally caught us with our pants down. They just didn't know when to quit. Even though they were the enemy, we have to marvel at their audacity and fighting spirit. The story had to be told.

I dedicate this book to the veterans of this conflict and to those who didn't come home. They wrote and acted in some of the most unbelievable scenarios in World War II. It was better than what Hollywood could ever produce!

Henry Sakaida

Temple City, California
August 15, 1995

## ACKNOWLEDGMENTS

This book would not have been possible without the help of many historians, veterans, and other contributors. First and foremost, I must thank the three individuals without whose help this book would not have been possible: Jiro Yoshida, a former Zero pilot and goodwill ambassador of the Zero Fighter Pilots Association, of Tokyo, Japan; David J. Duxbury, New Zealand aviation historian of Christchurch; and Commander Tomoyoshi Hori, the last executive officer of the 105th Naval Base Air Unit.

The numerous others are, in alphabetical order: Gensaku Aoki, Shigeo (Terao) Aso, John M. Arbuckle, Edward Benintende, Eric M. Bergerud, Angelo F. Bilotta, the late Captain Tom Blackburn, Steve Blake, the late Colonel Gregory "Pappy" Boyington, Ed Cornwell, Bryan B. Cox, David Enter, Minoru Fujita, Robert W. Griffith, Leo Harmon, Roland B. Heilman, Larry Hickey, Sig Higgins, the late Jose Holguin, Ralph Honda, William H. Hopper, Yoshiro Ikari, Yoshinobu Ikeda, Dr. Yasuho Izawa, Captain Robert J. Jones, Dr. Hugh D. Kennare, Sadamu Komachi, Major General Robert P. Keller, John W. Lambert (Phalanx Publishing), Jim Lansdale, Alexander "Lex" McAulay, Robert Millington, Masahiro Mitsuda, the late Yutaka Morioka, Roger Newton, Gary Nila, Ryoji Ohara, Masatake Okumiya, Hideo Ono, Robert K. Piper, Takeshi Saito, Saburo Sakai, Edward J. Shanley, Sekizen Shibayama, Yasushi Shimbo, Shiro Shimizu, Brantner Shraver, Ed Simmonds, Professor John Stephan, Shori Tanaka, Takeo Tanimizu, Barrett Tillman, Yoshikatsu Ushijima, Harold Venables, Fumio Wako, Robert W. Wilson, W. Raymond Woolrich, and Keizo Yamaguchi.

The following organizations also deserve to be mentioned: Australian Archives, Australian War Memorial, Kojinsha Co. (Maru Magazine), Marine Corps Aviation Association, National Archives, P-38 National Association, P.T. Boats Inc., Royal Australian Air Force, Royal New Zealand Air Force, Tailhook Association, Unabarakai (Association of former Japanese WII aviators), U.S. Air Force Historical Research Center, U.S. Marine Corps, U.S. Naval Historical Center, and the Veterans of Foreign Wars.

## TABLE OF CONTENTS

The 2 Nov. 1943 air attack on Rabaul, looking northeast over Lakunai A/D toward ships moored in Simpson Harbor. In the foreground, on the airstrip is a J1N1-S Irving nightfighter of the 251st Kokutai. On the edge of the field,from the lower left are two Ki-21 Sallys of the 14th Hiko Sentai, then under some camouflage netting a Sally of the 81st Hiko Sentai. IN the lower right is a Ki-46 Dinah of the 74th Independent Hiko Chutai. In the upper right hand corner an A6M5 Zero ( unit unknown ), its gear not yet retracted,climbs to meet the attackers. (Credit: National Archives via Jim Lansdale)

# 1

# THE WAR COMES TO RABAUL

Rabaul. The word evokes bitter memories that most surviving Japanese servicemen would rather forget. A sleepy copra port town on an island in the Southwest Pacific, very few had ever heard of it before the war. To the Japanese, it was a giant aerial meat grinder, the "Russian Front" of the South Pacific. The town of Rabaul is located on Gazelle Peninsula, on the northeastern part of New Britain Island. During World War II, it became the most important Japanese air base in the Southwest Pacific. Japanese aircrews referred to it as the Graveyard of Fighter Pilots.[1] Assignment to Rabaul in 1943-44 was a virtual death sentence.

It was a hornet's nest that could also impart a lethal sting to Allied aircrews. Prior to the war, Rabaul boasted having one of the best natural harbors in the South Pacific handling over 300,000 tons of freight each year. Over a hundred coconut plantations sent their copra (dried coconut meat used to make oil) to Rabaul's Simpson Harbor for export. Because of its location, it became the cultural and commercial center for Gazelle Peninsula. The native population were Melanesians; Europeans and Chinese, with a smattering of other nationalities, ran the commerce.

The area surrounding Rabaul has a climate of mild seasonal variations with annual rainfall of about ninety inches; mean annual temperature is eighty-two degrees.[2] It wasn't exactly a tourist Mecca, but it was serene. Rabaul's port and strategic location in the Solomon's did not go unnoticed to the Japanese in far-off Tokyo. Rabaul was in the wrong geographical location at the wrong time. Its attributes were enticing - a large native work force, developed agriculture to sustain an occupying force and an airfield.

By the fall of 1941 the China War was going nowhere; the Japanese and the Chinese were in a stalemate. Although the invaders could not possibly conquer all of China, they held most of the important cities and ports. The Russians, to the north, were kept in check with the recently signed non-aggression pact. The British, French, Dutch, and the Russians were preoccupied with the gigantic battles in Europe. The Americans lacked influence in this part of the world, therefore the situation was ripe for the Japanese to expand their empire, obtain the petroleum fields of the Dutch East Indies, and drive out the Westerners. As part of the overall Japanese strategy the capture of Rabaul would impede Allied supply efforts to New Zealand, New Guinea, and Australia and cause them to fall like dominoes.

With lightning-like precision the Japanese struck simultaneously at Pearl Harbor, the Philippines, Hong Kong, and Malaya on 7 December 1941 - the start of the Pacific War. Guam and Wake Island fell to the invaders by the end of December; Singapore was under siege. Rabaul was about to be steamrolled.

The entire defense of the Bismarck Archipelago and the Solomon Islands rested upon the Australians, who with the bulk of their Army engaged in North Africa, were ill-prepared to fight a Pacific war. Ground troops in New Britain amounted to no more than 1,400 men. The Royal Australian Air Force had a handful of Lockheed Hudson bombers based at Vunakanau (West

**Mitsubishi A6M2 Model 21 Zeros preparing for take-off from Rabaul in 1943. (Credit: Maru)**

A closer view of parafrags raining down on Vunakanau Airfield, 12 Oct 43. (Credit: J.C. Hanna)

Airfield) and some Wirraways (license-produced North American AT-6s) at Lakunai (East Airfield.)[3]

The conquest of Rabaul began with a warm-up bombing attack against Lakunai. Eighteen four-engine Mavis flying boats dropped bombs which caused very little physical damage but much psychological hurt. After a few more raids in December and January, the jittery Aussies withdrew their Hudsons. With the RAAF out of the way, the Japanese sent a convoy of ships through St. George's Channel toward Rabaul on 22 January 1942. They were supported by aircraft from Truk Island and Admiral Nagumo's carrier force. Australian defenders could do little to hamper the enemy's landing schedule. Rabaul fell the next day and the Japanese began operating naval aircraft out of Lakunai Airfield. Kavieng, on the northern tip of New Ireland Island, also fell, and both Rabaul and Kavieng became strongholds for the Japanese Army.

To protect the newly arrived garrisons on Rabaul and Kavieng, the Japanese brought in elements of the 11th Air Fleet. The first fighter aircraft were the Type 96s - open cockpit, fixed-landing gear workhorses (and borderline relics) from the China War. Lieutenant Harutoshi Okamoto and his carrier pilots from the Chitose Air Group landed on 31 January, slightly behind another smaller contingent which had arrived days earlier. The Tainan Naval Air Group arrived at Rabaul in mid-April 1942 and shuttled between there and Lae. The latter unit was famous for having the highest number of "aces." They were followed in turn by Mitsubishi Zeroes from the 1st Air Group and other units.

Rabaul served as a staging area for attacks on New Guinea and the Solomons, Japanese aircraft first engaging Allied Forces in the Battle of the Coral Sea during May. The outcome of this historic carrier duel caused the Japanese to abandon the idea of landing forces at Port Moresby. After the Battle of Midway in June 1942, Japan was forced into a defensive mode. At this time, there were sixty Zero fighters based at Rabaul, plus an equal number of twin-engine Betty and Nell bombers, twenty-seven float planes, and six flying boats.[4] Counter attacking Allied forces invaded Guadalcanal on 7 August 1942 prompting Rabaul to reply with Betty bombers and Zero escorts. The bombing raids were ineffective, the Japanese suffering heavy casualties on these long range missions, and a series of costly land and sea battles also failed to dislodge the Allied beachhead on Guadalcanal. On 9 November, the Japanese attempted to land 12,000 men and supplies (eleven transport ships) on the island. During the Naval Battle of Guadalcanal (14-15 November), seven of the Japanese troop transports were sunk by American aircraft. Only 4,000 men and less than five tons of supplies were landed. On 25 December 1942, Imperial Headquarters ordered Rabaul HQ to abandon their plans to retake Guadalcanal.[5] The price of the Guadalcanal Campaign for the Japanese was exorbitant: over 25,000 men and about 600 aircraft had been lost. Their Army was also faring badly in New Guinea.

1. Statements from former Zero pilot Masahiro Mitsuda, as well as surviving Rabaul veterans Sadamu Komachi and Takeo Tanimizu, 1981.

2. *United States Strategic Bombing Survey* (Pacific), The Allied Campaign Against Rabaul, Naval Analysis Division, 1 September 1946, 4-5.

3. Ibid., 6.

4. Ibid., 8.

5. Ibid., 9.

# 2

# 1943 - THE TURNING POINT

The Kanoya Naval Air Group, progenitor of Rabaul's last Zero squadron, was established on 1 April 1936 at Kanoya on Kyushu Island, Japan. It cut its combat teeth in the China War and later participated in the Malayan Campaign, gaining fame for the sinking of the British battleship *Prince of Wales* and the cruiser *Repulse*.[1]

The unit proceeded to Rabaul in September 1942 and carried out attacks on Allied beachheads in the Solomons and New Guinea. On 1 November, it was split into two groups; one became the 751st Air Group (bombers) while the other was designated the 253rd Air Group (A6M2 Zero fighters). Commander Yoshito Kobayashi served as the new fighter unit commander until July 1943, when he was replaced by Commander Taro Fukuda. The 253rd pulled back to Truk to reorganize and refit, then came back to Rabaul's East Airfield (Tobera) for an encore. It replaced the 201st and 204th Air Groups which had been cut to pieces.

The first Japanese Army Air Force unit to arrive at Rabaul was the 11th Fighter Regiment. It gained famed during the 1939 Khalkin Gol (Nomonhan) Campaign against the Russians on the Soviet-Manchurian border where, in three months of intense combat, they claimed over 530 aerial victories. On 18 December 1942, they landed at Vunakanau Airfield.[2] Next came the 1st Fighter Regiment, another Kalkin Gol veteran, on 9 January 1943. The 68th, armed with their new Ki-61 Hien (Tony) fighters, arrived at the end of April 1943, followed by the 78th two months later.

The Japanese Army had their priorities in New Guinea; their ground troops needed air support which the Navy could not or would not provide. There was very little cooperation between the Army and Navy at Rabaul, or elsewhere. Thus Rabaul's Army Air Regiments achieved very little success, and by the end of August 1943, almost all of the Army fighters had been transferred to Lae and Wewak. If Rabaul was the Graveyard of Fighter Pilots, New Guinea was the Army's.

The 1st and 11th Fighter Regiments were eventually withdrawn from New Guinea during the summer of 1943 after horrendous losses. Those units remaining (68th, 77th, 78th, and 248th) were virtually annihilated and were disbanded on 25 July 1944. Some pilots and groundcrews stayed behind to fight as infantrymen.[3]

Rabaul was another matter. The punitive daylight bombardment campaign against Rabaul began on 12 October 1943. This was a momentous strike and General George Kenney, leading the Fifth Air Force, wanted to make a lasting first impression. Over 350 aircraft and 300 tons of bombs caught the enemy's undivided attention. Another raid followed six days later, followed by relentless subsequent Allied attacks.

The Zero pilots on Rabaul were eventually caught in a no-win situation. Their aircraft were ultimately outnumbered and outclassed in performance by the Vought F4U Corsair, Grumman F6F Hellcat and the Lockheed P-38 Lightning. Of these three types of American aircraft, the Japanese pilots considered the Corsair to be the most troublesome, due to its superior

An A6M5 Model 52 Mitsubishi Zero (Zeke in Allied code terms) of the 253rd Air Group based at Tobera. It sports the victory and tail markings of their top pilot CPO Tetsuzo Iwamoto. (Depiction by Shori Tanaka)

The Grumman F6F Hellcat, a factory fresh model in 1943. (Credit: Lambert)

speed. The Hellcat was not as fast as the F4U "Whistling Death," but it was much more maneuverable.[4] P-38s were initially easy prey until their pilots learned how to maximize their high altitude performance and developed hit and run tactics.

Rabaul started receiving the newest model of the standard Zero, the A6M5 Model 52s in late 1943. The Model 52 had a maximum speed of 351 mph at 19,685 feet. It was a slight improvement over the earlier Model 21s (331 mph maximum). In comparison to the Allied fighters, the deadly Zero of 1941-42 fame had become obsolete. The Grumman F6F-3's maximum speed was 375 mph at 17,300 feet. The twin-boom P-38 was slightly faster at 390 mph (25,000 feet). The F4U-1 Corsair's top speed of 417 mph at 19,900 feet literally took the Japanese pilots' breathe away. Strange as it may seem, some of the old pros amongst the Zero pilots still preferred the old 21s, which was about 600 pounds lighter than the 52s. Those 600 pounds meant the difference between life and death in a maneuvering battle.

The Japanese warrior code of Bushido demanded that they fight offensively at all times. This meant enticing or luring unsuspecting Allied pilots into close quarter dogfighting where the Japanese could outturn their opponent. Japanese pilots themselves demanded maneuverability over armor protection, the latter adding weight to their aircraft, compromising maneuverability and range.[5]

Unknown to the Japanese, their counterparts had become very knowledgeable about the Zero, having captured an intact A6M2 in the Aleutians in 1942. Aircraft engineers and test pilots wrung the secrets out of it and the mysterious Zero fighter had lost its allure.

The Zero's light construction was a great asset, but it was also was its greatest liability. The heavier American fighters could out dive it and escape. With no self-sealing fuel tanks, strategic hits were enough to ignite the Zero. Allied fighter pilots recognized these weaknesses and engaged in coordinated hit and run tactics. They were warned never to engage in close quarter dogfighting, and those who foolishly broke this cardinal rule of engagement usually paid with their lives.

Petty Officer Sadamu Komachi of the 253rd hated the Grummans. Komachi was a veteran of Hawaii, Indian Ocean, Coral Sea and Solomons battles and an accomplished carrier pilot. A modest individual, his peers attribute over forty aerial victories to him, and he was one of the very few veterans to survive. "The Grummans would get on your tail and just shower you with bullets!" he complained. "It was just awful. I wish we had six .50s like the Grummans and Corsairs!"[6]

General Kenny introduced his Army P-38 Lightnings to the Rabaul Campaign on 2 November 1943. The 39th and 80th Squadrons were ordered to precede B-25s and sweep away any opposition over Simpson Harbor and Lakunai Airfield as the Fifth Air Force bombed Rabaul in support of the landings on Bougainville Island.

The Japanese scrambled 112 Zero fighters to oppose the seventy-eight B-25s and P-38 escorts. Aerial burst bombs were dropped over the Mitchell formations, but failed to have any effect. The Fifth Air Force claimed forty enemy fighters shot down while nine Lightnings and nine Mitchells failed to return. The Japanese

Ace Sadamu Komachi, a veteran carrier pilot. (Credit: S. Komachi)

The formidable Vought Corsair, this one belonging to VMF-222, at Bougainville in April 1944. (Credit: Tailhook)

claimed an incredible 119 aerial victories and actually lost eighteen fighters.[7]

Petty Officer Takeo Tanimizu, a carrier pilot on temporary duty at Rabaul, flew with the 253rd on this day. It was his baptism of fire and he claimed two Lightnings. He went on to claim over 32 victories at war's end. "The P-38s at lower altitudes were easy prey," he comments. "They were not very fast, so they usually stayed at higher altitudes. Then, they'd swoop down on you, fire, and zoom up. You really had to be careful and keep looking up. Their weakest spot was their tail. A 20mm hit and their tails would snap off."[8]

Sixteen Zeroes from the 281st Air Group touched down on the dusty airfield at Tobera on 14 November 1943. The flight leader, twenty-seven year old Chief Petty Officer Tetsuzo Iwamoto, was warmly welcomed by Commander Takeo Shibata. The two had fought together during the China War. On his first mission on 25 February 1938, Iwamoto had shot down five enemy aircraft. He became the top Navy scorer in China with fourteen victories. Iwamoto and the US Navy's VF-17 were about to clash.

Fighting 17 was one of the US Navy's shore-based fighter squadrons employed against the Japanese at Rabaul. Calling themselves "Jolly Rogers," the

PO Takeo Tanimizu, May 1942 aboard aircraft carrier *Junyo*. (Credit: Tanimizu)

Japan's top Navy ace in WW II, Tetsuzo Iwamoto, as an ensign in 1945. (Credit: Y. Izawa)

The pilots in this VF-17 photo represent 41 victories. Taken at Ondongo in Nov 1943, the "Jolly Rogers" are: (L. to R.) Earl May, Clement Gile, Robert Hogan, Tom Blackburn (wearing hat), Basil Henning, Brad Baker (holding pith helmet), Walter Schub, Robert Jackson, Robert Anderson and Lyle Hermann. (Credit: Tom Blackburn)

F4Us sported the skull and crossbones on their engine cowlings and were led by the charismatic Lieutenant Commander Tommy Blackburn. Competition between VF-17 and the Marine's VMF-214 "Blacksheep" was fierce. Their leaders were as different as night and day. Major Gregory "Pappy" Boyington CO of VMF-214 was a tough, burly ex-Flying Tiger veteran, unconventional and crude. Blackburn was a savvy and aggressive gentleman/businessman. His business was to draw and quarter aerial opponents (his personal score was 11 victories).

After the Americans waded ashore on Torokina (Bougainville Island) on 1 November 1943 the Japanese responded with all available units on 17 November utilizing seventy single-engined bombers and over forty Zero escorts.[9]

Petty Officer Iwamoto and his newly arrived contingent brought up the rear of the massive strike force. Most of his pilots were neophytes straight from Japan, and this would be their first combat. As the bombers climbed to 24,000 feet, Iwamoto and his men, still flying old Model 21s, were hard pressed to keep up. He wrote in his diary:

> "With this antiquated plane we were expected to fight against the enemy's latest models that vastly outnumbered us. It was like being ordered to die. We had no choice but to obey orders and do our best."[10]

Eight VF-17 Corsairs were patrolling over Empress Augusta Bay at 25,000 feet when ground control radioed that bogeys were in-coming. Suddenly, Lieu-

tenant Clement Gile gave the Tallyho: "Bandits at two o'clock, thirty degrees down. Twelve Zekes right over eight Kates."

Petty Officer Iwamoto watched helplessly as the Corsairs dove into the flight of Zeroes ahead. Lieutenant Commander Roger Hedrick took out the flight leader and Lieutenant (j.g.) Mills Schanuel knocked down the wingman. Lieutenant Paul Cordray went after the Kates (torpedo planes) and flamed one.[11]

As the Japanese escort reacted Lieutenant (j.g.) Robert S. Anderson was set upon by a pair of Japanese veterans; one whipped around on his tail and delivered telling hits. Anderson pulled up and lost his attacker but was forced to bail out when his left wing caught fire and smoke filled his cockpit.

Iwamoto noted: "The American planes were the new F4U Sikorskys...I shot down an F4U in a single pass, then climbed up and attacked the plane that was behind the first one. This one was not so easy and he wouldn't give up. We each fought fiercely and finally I won."[12]

The Japanese attack on Torokina was unsuccessful. Two Zero pilots from the 204th (Petty Officers Junji Kato and Kiyoshi Yamakawa) and three from the 201st (Ensign Yukio Aiso and Petty Officers Jisuke Yoshino and Takeo Shigegaki) failed to return. The 201st claimed two F4Us, but overall Japanese claims are unknown. Iwamoto was very bitter about the losses which he attributed to the inexperienced mission leader.

VF-17 lost two Corsairs and one pilot, their first casualties in combat. Bob Anderson was picked up by

A panoramic view of Simpson Harbor as seen from a 498th Bomb Sq. B-25 on 2 Nov 1943. Parafrag bombs can just be seen floating down on Rabaul City. (Credit: Thomas K. Lewis)

a PT boat, but Ensign Bradford W. Baker disappeared in the fierce combat and never returned. Corsair pilots claimed ten victories in this encounter, three Zeroes by Dexter Gile.

Four days later (21 November), Iwamoto and VF-17 clashed again over Empress Augusta Bay. The Japanese failed in their attempt to knock out the airfield and two pilots failed to return (Petty Officers Yorihisa Kobayashi and Shotaku Yamaguchi). VF-17 claimed six Zeroes and suffered no losses. Iwamoto was very impressed with Blackburn's "Jolly Rogers" and noted in his diary: "These Americans were fine fighters."[13]

December 17, 1943 marked the first time that Allied land-based single-engine fighters appeared over Rabaul, an ominous sign for the Japanese. This intrusion had been made possible by the capture of Torokina on Bougainville Island.

Major Greg Boyington, commanding officer of VMF-214, was selected to lead the fighter sweep. Major General Ralph J. "Pete" Mitchell USMC personally selected "Blacksheep One" for his prowess, but the honoree felt dubious about leading seventy-six aircraft. As Boyington would later recall, "The Allied fighters were of so many different types, we might just as well have been escorting bombers. Because the five large airfields on New Britain and New Ireland were spread over a large area, the mission at least should have been restricted to fighters with the same flying characteristics."[14] Thirty-one Corsairs, twenty-three P-40s, and twenty-two Hellcats were not a homogeneous mix.

Wing Commander Trevor Owen Freeman and his P-40s (14 and 16 Squadrons, RNZAF) were the first to take off. They made a beeline to Rabaul and never

looked back, arriving minutes before the Americans could get into high cover position. It would prove to be a costly mistake. As the Kiwis crossed over Gazelle Peninsula from Kabanga Bay, about 20 miles southeast of Rabaul, they noticed dust over the various airfields – evidence that Zeroes had taken off. The enemy was lurking nearby, but the New Zealanders were confident and spoiling for a fight.

The Kittyhawks ran into a patrol of twelve Zeroes from the 204th Air Group, led by Ensign Ito. They were joined by fifteen Zeroes from the 201st and then the 253rd entered the slugfest. The Japanese swarmed over the New Zealanders. Freeman, unabashed by the odds, dispatched a Zero and added insult to injury by yelling into the radio "Tojo eats Spam, Tojo eats Spam!"

By the time the American fighters arrived on the scene, it was one giant free-for-all. VMF-214's First Lieutenant Robert W. McClurg claimed a Rufe single-float seaplane fighter over Simpson Harbor while his comrade Donald Jay Moore claimed two Zeroes. Boyington felt left out and resorted to the radio, inviting his opponents to come up and fight.

"Come on down, sucker!" came the retort over Boyington's receiver.[15] The Allied radio transmissions were being monitored by four Niseis (second generation Japanese-Americans) at Rabaul HQ. These civilian translators had learned the American lingo in the good old US of A.[16]

The 201st and 204th jointly claimed fifteen victories (mostly over the P-40s) plus two Hellcats; their only casualty being Petty Office Second Class Isamu Koyama (204th). While the claims of the 253rd are unknown, they did loose one aircraft. A young 18 year old

Flight Seaman 3/c Masajiro Kawato in Japan just prior to his departure for Rabaul. (Credit: M. Kawato)

named Masajiro Kawato collided with Flight Lieutenant John O. McFarlane's P-40. Both parachuted into the harbor and were rescued.

Wing Commander Freeman and his wingman, Flight Sergeant E.C. Laurie, jumped eight or nine Zeroes over Praed Point; each claimed a Zero, but Freeman sustained hits. Streaming smoke or glycol, he became separated from his comrade and attracted undue attention. Seven or eight Zeroes joined in the "feeding frenzy." Two Kittyhawks then jumped in to affect a rescue and the three of them raced towards New Ireland. Freeman circled a valley, looking for a clearing to land as his wingmen kept guard. The Zeroes soon arrived and his comrades were forced to scatter. Freeman was never seen again. The New Zealanders claimed a total of six Zeroes shot down in the day's fighting.[17]

The Hellcats did well. Ensign Frank Edward Schneider of VF-33 claiming a Zero over St. George's Channel while all returned safely to base.

The first land-based single-engine fighter sweep over Rabaul had been a sobering experience for General Mitchell and his staff. Recalled Boyington, "This mass boober was just another thing in my life I couldn't be proud of..."[18]

However, the daily grind of combat and the Allied superiority in numbers began to take its toll on the Zero pilots. From 17 December until the New Year, the Marines pummeled Rabaul with a vengeance. Petty Officer Iwamoto was tired and disgusted. Despite his vast experience, he was now constantly in danger of being overwhelmed. There were sixty cherry blossoms painted on the side of his Zero, denoting the number of enemy aircraft he had claimed shot down. While individual victory scores were not officially recognized, pilots did keep score. He would eventually claim 142 of his 202 aerial victories over Rabaul.[19]

The magnitude of the false propaganda being fed to the people in Japan would have made those in Rabaul angry. A jovial news crew came to film pilots for the folks back home and were surprised to encounter sullen faces and an icy atmosphere. When they asked if any pilot was willing to mount a movie camera on the wing of their fighters to record their combat missions, there was an astounding, "No!"[20] It had been planned that the aerial camera would be mounted externally on top of the wing but pilots were fearful of comprising a little speed induced by its drag.

Iwamoto noted in his diary: "Prior to the beginning of 1943, we still had hope and fought fiercely. But now, we fought to uphold our honor. We didn't want to become cowards...We believed that we were expendable, that we were all going to die. There was no hope of survival - no one cared anymore."[21]

According to Japanese Naval records, from October 1942 until February 1944, 1,357 Allied fighters were shot down by their pilots in the Solomons, plus 611 light bombers and fifty medium and heavy bombers.[22] The score keeping was obviously flawed. The pilots' claims were taken on face value and there was no reason to inflate them. Unlike the Allied fighter pilots who became "aces" after shooting down five or more enemy fighters, the Japanese pilot received no such status. All victories since June 1943 were credited to the squadron. But that didn't stop pilots like Iwamoto from painting their scores on aircraft. It was done for morale purposes. There were no medals, promotions, or even publicity for shooting down a score of enemy aircraft – it was simply a part of their duty.

The astronomical claims delighted Imperial Headquarters back in Tokyo and they may have believed them, but the men on the front lines knew better. Rather than boosting morale, such self-serving propaganda steadily eroded it. Broken in spirit and health, many Japanese aviators found their solace in death.

1. Ikuhiko Hata and Yasuho Izawa, *Japanese Naval Aces and Fighter Units in World War II*, Naval Institute Press, 1989, 160.
2. Ikuhiko Hata and Yasuho Izawa, *Nippon Rikugun Sentoki Tai* (Japanese Army Fighter Regiments, Kantosha Publishers, Tokyo, Japan, 1977, 46,48.
3. Ibid., respective unit histories.
4. *U.S.S.B.S.*, 22.
5. Interviews with former Zero pilots Masahiro Mitsuda, Takeo Tanimizu, Sadamu Komachi, Saburo Sakai, and Yutaka Morioka, Japan, 1979-1981.
6. Interview with Sadamu Komachi, Tokyo, Japan, November 1981.

14

7. *Japanese Naval Aces and Fighter Units* Appendix D, Major Air Battles by Date, 430

8. Interview with Takeo Tanimizu, Osaka, Japan, November 1981.

9. Flight log of 204 Air Group, 17 November 1943. According to Tetsuzo Iwamoto's memoir, the numbers were 20 land attack planes (single-engine bombers) and 60 Zero escorts. However, I believe the 204 Air Group's flight log is correct.

10. Tetsuzo Iwamoto, *Zero-Sen Gekitsui O* (Shoot Down King of Zero Fighter), Konnichi No Wadai Publishers, Tokyo, Japan, 1972.

11. Tom Blackburn, *The Jolly Rogers, The Story of Tom Blackburn and Navy Fighting Squadron VF-17*, Orion Books, New York, 1989, 157.

12. *Zero-Sen Gekitsui O.*

13. Ibid. Iwamoto kept an elaborate notebook during the war. However, some notes of particular aerial combat missions were not recorded until a length of time had passed. Hence, he was off on some dates and some circumstances were mingled with others. Japanese Navy records list Petty Officers Yorihisa Kobayashi and Shotaku Yamaguchi as killed on 22 November 1943. However, there were no fighter claims by F4Us that day. In this case, Japanese records are a day off, which is not unusual.

14. The 71st Seabees labored around the clock to construct an airstrip. On 10 December, seventeen Corsairs of newly arrived VMF-216 were the first to touch down, followed by six SBD Dauntless dive bombers and four transports.

15. Colonel Gregory "Pappy" Boyington, *Baa Baa Blacksheep*, Bantam Books edition, 1977, 202.

16. ComAir Sols Fighter Command War Diary, December 1943

17. The Japanese Naval Headquarters at Rabaul employed at least four American-born citizens of Japanese descent. It was common for Japanese families in the United States to send their eldest sons back to Japan for a formal Japanese education. When the war broke out, they could not return home. They were conscripted into the military as civilian interpreters. They monitored Allied radio transmissions and helped interrogate captured aviators. Hori told me about them in 1993 and their existence was confirmed through an Australian report on suspected Japanese war crimes. The four Niseis were Masayuki Takamoto, Tadashi Mizokawa, Edward Chikaki Honda, and Jun Kawasaki.

18. Squadron Leader J.M.S. Ross, *Royal New Zealand Air Force*, War History Branch, Wellington, New Zealand. Also, biographical information on McFarlane and Freeman from Ministry of Defence, Wellington, New Zealand, 1987.

19. *Baa Baa Blacksheep*, 203.

20. *Zero-Sen Gekitsui O*. According to Iwamoto's reckoning, his claims included 202 destroyed in the air, 26 shared, 22 uncertain, two damaged, and two burned on the ground. His grand total is 254 aircraft destroyed or damaged. Some of his claims were: F4F x7, P-38 x 4, F4U x 48 (one uncertain), P-40 x 1, P-39 x 2, F6F x 29, SBD x 48, and B-25 x 8. In addition, he claimed another 30 SBDs by aerial burst bombs. His victory claims are hyperinflated due to confusion in combat and a very loose method of accounting. Iwamoto died in 1955 as a result of a botched surgical operation on his back.

21. Ibid.

22. Ibid.

23. *U.S.S.B.S.*, 54

The 253rd Air Group poses at Tobera Airfield in Feb 1944. Some of the pilots were: Masajiro Kawato (front row, 5th from left). Second row: 3rd from left Tetsutaro Kumagaya, unknown, LCDR Harutoshi Okamoto, CDR Taro Fukuda (in pith helmet), Torajiro Haruta, Tetsuzo Iwamoto, Shigeo Fukumoto, Sadamu Komachi, Kaoru Takaiwa, and Kingo Seo (standing). Third row: (L. to R.) Sekizen Shibayama, Yoshio Otsuki, Gensaku Aoki, (7th from left) Yoshinobu Ikeda, (13th from left). Fourth row: (L. to R.) Takashi Kaneko, Ken-Ichi Takahashi (7th from left) and Kentaro Miyagoshi (far right). (Credit: Sekizen Shibayama)

# 3

# WAR OF ATTRITION

The New Year started out with a bang – literally. US carrier aircraft tortured Kavieng on the northern tip of New Ireland Island as VF-18 Hellcats from *Bunker Hill* chalked up the first victories for 1944. Working together with VF-30 from *Monterey*, the Americans claimed twelve Zeroes shot down with eleven probables.

Fifteen B-24s of the Thirteenth Air Force, escorted by Grumman F6Fs, bombed Rabaul's Lakunai Airfield. Opposition was pitiful. The 204th Air Group could muster only eight aircraft to oppose the raid losing Petty Officer First Class Tsuneo Suzuki. Bomber gunners put in outlandish claims for twenty-five Zeroes shot down while the Hellcat pilots recorded three victories and two probables. The 201st Air Group scrambled four aircraft and lost Petty Officer Michio Takeshita.

While the 201st and the 204th were busy over Rabaul, the 253rd's twenty-eight Zero fighters, led by Lieutenant Kenji Nakagawa, were trying to bomb and strafe enemy shipping at Marcus Bay in the Arawe area. They set fire to two vessels and sustained minor damage to one aircraft.[1]

Within the Marine Corps and the Fifth Air Force there was a scoring race to see who would break Eddie Rickenbacker's WW I record of twenty-six victories. Marine ace Captain Joe Foss of VMF-121 had tied it and many believed that the number was cursed. Many bets were on Major Gregory "Pappy" Boyington, commanding officer of VMF-214 who was thoroughly professional in his approach to aerial combat and never attempted to force success. He tried to ignore the pressure, but two victories shy of a new record, he was reportedly more irritable than usual.

Three days into the New Year, Boyington and his wingman, Captain George Ashmun, were last seen hurling themselves at the enemy over the St. George's Channel off the coast of New Ireland. He and Ashmun became separated from their flock in the clouds, then were pounced upon by over twenty Zeroes. Boyington claimed three Zeroes and confirmed one for his wingman, but Ashmun was hit and went down in a half glide with the enemy wailing on him.[2]

In a desperate attempt to run interference, Boyington skidded his Corsair from side to side, spraying the Japanese to no avail. Four Zeroes followed him down and achieved the near impossible by igniting the Corsair's fuel tanks.[3] The old pro parachuted out of his burning crate at low altitude and was slammed violently into the water seconds after his chute deployed. His victors then amused themselves by strafing him in the water, but he was not hit.[4]

"I ended up in the water almost abreast of Cape St. George, New Ireland, about five miles from shore,"

**Mechanics labor over an A6M Zero at Lakunai Airfield. In the background is Mt. Hanabuki which erupted in Sep. 1994 dumping tons of ash on downtown Rabaul and Lakunai. (Credit: Maru)**

recalled Boyington. "I knew we had a coast watcher at this point and had high hopes of having him rescue me." The coast watcher never materialized, but a Japanese submarine did and Boyington was hauled aboard while his hosts served him refreshments and cigarettes on their surface trip to Rabaul.[5]

Seventy Zeroes from the 204th and 253rd had been engaged in combat with Corsairs that day, claiming a total of eight F4Us destroyed with three probables.[6] American claims by both F4U and F6F pilots were nine victories and four probables. However, the only recorded losses that day were Boyington and Ashmun from VMF-214, and Petty Officers Hideshi Tanimoto and Yoshige Kitade, both from the 204th.

The disappearance of Boyington on 3 January 1944 sent shock waves through the Marine Corps and the American public. Captain John Foster of VMF-222 remarked: "If the Japs had been able to get Gregory Boyington – the man, above all men, who knew what to expect from a Jap in a fight, who had learned during four long dangerous years how to hate and how to avenge that hate – then what was the chance for the rest of us, who were rank amateurs by comparison? None of us believed he was lost for good. He was too tough, too hickory-like."[7]

The following day, the Marines sent at least four squadrons over Rabaul while the Navy contributed VF-40 Hellcats. Twenty-seven Zeroes of the 204th, led by Lieutenant Yamaguchi, fought an estimated twenty-two F4Us and F6Fs, claiming eight Corsairs and two Hellcats destroyed. Their only casualty was Petty Officer Koichi Kubota. The 253rd sortied twenty-seven Zeroes, claimed eight Corsairs downed, and suffered two pilots killed (Petty Officers Ryosuke Baba and Hiroshi Kuwahara) and three aircraft damaged. There was only one American loss that day, Captain Harvey F. Carter.

Carter would have remained a forgotten figure, one of many who went missing and became a statistic, had it not been for one particular Zero pilot - Petty Officer Takeo Tanimizu of the 253rd. Tanimizu, an experienced veteran, had come to Rabaul in November 1943 as part of a detachment from the First Carrier Division. Carter was one of eight pilots from VMF-321 assigned to a fifty-six plane fighter sweep over Rabaul. The unit was led by Captain Rolland S. Mangel, with Carter leading the second division composed of First Lieutenants William Crapo, George B. Dixon Jr., and Second Lieutenant Robert Whiting. Carter had received his commission on 27 May 1942 in Saskatchewan, Canada and had joined VMF-321 in San Diego, California.

VMF-321 mission report provides the following details:

"Eight F4U's from VMF-321 left on course at 1200 under the leadership of Captain Mangel. Over Cape St. George, up channel into Simpson Harbor, arriving on station at 1300, at 25,000 feet. The entire group made one complete sweep around Simpson Harbor before making

VMF-321 pilots on Efate Island, December 1943. Capt. Marion McCown is standing fourth from the left and Capt. Harvey Carter is standing fourth from right. (Credit: Leo Harmon)

Vice Adm. Jin-Ichi Kusaka, Commander, Eleventh Air Fleet, in his underground HQ at Rabaul in 1944. (Credit: Naotaro Kusaka)

contact. When the rest of the formation dropped lower, Capt. Mangel's division sighted twelve Zekes coming up through cloud cover at 21,000 ft. The division however, did not make contact. Carter's division made contact at approx. 21,000 ft. Whiting scored one sure Zeke. Dixon who had left because his oxygen gave out before entering Simpson Harbor, contacted three Zekes over Cape St. George on his way home knocking down two sures. Capt. Carter did not return from the mission. He was last seen by his wingman, Lt. Whiting at 21,000 ft. over the southern edge of Simpson Harbor. He was apparently in no trouble at the time."[8]

Petty Officer Takeo Tanimizu, after the conclusion of combat, was in the vicinity of Cape St. George when he noticed a parachute floating down into the sea. It was Captain Harvey F. Carter. Apparently hit in combat, he bailed out, unseen by his comrades. Tanimizu felt pity for this pilot and flew down low. Carter splashed down and was seen bobbing in the water. The Zero circled the downed pilot and Tanimizu opened his cockpit and tossed out a life ring. It landed close to the American and Carter swam to it. He acknowledged the gift with a hearty wave. Tanimizu circled Carter, then set course for base.[9]

When Carter failed to return, a Dumbo was sent aloft with sixteen escorts at 1615. They returned at 1830 with no success. Leo Harmon describes the rescue effort:

"You will note that later that afternoon, we escorted Dumbo (PBY-5) back to the Cape St. George area in search of any downed airmen, and found nothing. It would be of interest to know just where the Japanese pilot dropped his buoy and pinpoint the exact location of the downed pilot since we sent sixteen Corsairs along with the Dumbo aircraft which had a trained aircrew. It is possible that we may not have gone far enough North, or the downed pilot may have been too close to Cape St. George where there were heavy anti-aircraft installations. If we had spotted anyone, we would have attempted to rescue him."

"Since we always sent the Dumbo on a search mission to the area after downed aircrewmen, it is difficult to understand how we could have missed seeing anyone in the water provided that the downed pilot used the equipment he carried with him. It is possible the pilot went ashore at Cape St. George, in which case he could have been captured by the Japanese ground forces in the area."

"As I recall," remembers Harmon, "Carter wore a mustache and had the air of an Englishman. He was a good pilot and I was told, had the distinction of flying loops around a bridge over the Mississippi River near New Orleans where he was an instructor at a Navy training base. I met Carter's parents who drove us from Los Angeles to San Diego the day we boarded the carrier on our way to Samoa in Sept. 1943."

"Sometime in 1946, I visited Carter's parents at their home in Verdugo City, California and talked with them for a short time. There wasn't much that I could tell them that they didn't already know, and I felt at a loss for words to

An aerial view of the 11 Nov. 1943 attack on Japanese shipping in Rabaul's Simpson Harbor. (Credit: USN)

express my feelings in the matter. Mr. Carter thanked me for visiting them and said he would call me and invite me to dinner sometime, but I never heard from them after that."[10]

Despite the ferocity of the air battles over Rabaul, the American pilots retained their great sense of humor. Combat stories became taller and more unbelievable with each retelling. Some of it was true. Robert Griffith, a former pilot in VMF-321, recalls an incident involving a comrade: "We had a Captain McCown in VMF-321. He and his wingman were coming home from Rabaul one day and were strafing the airfield at Buka. Rabaul was clouded over and Buka was the secondary target."

"Wingman Bob See made the first strafing run without return fire but when McCown made his run, he was hit by machine gun fire and was forced to make a water landing nearby. Afraid to swim ashore at Buka, he was able to find an underwater reef that he could stand on, shoulder deep. Hopeful that Dumbo would pick him up that same afternoon, he was satisfied to just stand still. Until!"

"A shark appeared on the scene and circled McCown. Each circle a bit closer until he gently put his nose on Mac's behind and pushed him off the reef. In panic, McCown scrambled back on the reef only to be pushed off again. This happened several times, according to McCown, until the shark tired of the game and left. We got McCown back the next morning and the skipper promptly gave him the day off (joke)."[11]

Captain Marion R. McCown Jr.'s last mission and his disappearance gave credence to a rumor that the Japanese had captured a Corsair and used it to stalk unsuspecting Americans. Five days after his shark encounter, on 15 January 1944, the 27 year old Charleston, South Carolina native flew a B-25 escort mission to Rabaul. Captain McCown flew in Lieutenant Robert See's division of four F4Us (See, McCown, and First Lieutenants Robert Hugh Brindos and R.W. Marshall). While flying top cover over the bombers, south of Cape St. George, they ran into the entire 204th Air Group (42 Zeroes). The Japanese were soon crawling over them. See managed to claim two Zeroes and returned safely to base, but the other three disappeared. Brindos was captured two days later.[12]

Bob Griffith writes:

"Because of the 'no prisoner' policy of both the Japanese and ourselves, it was always joked that if one got shot down near the enemy's airfield - 'Head for the landing strip, make a wheels up landing and run for the commanding officer's tent.

"Wouldn't you know, he was knocked down right over the target and was last seen stirring up a long cloud of dust on one of the runways. A few days later we heard that Tokyo Rose reported Captain McCown was on his way to Tokyo. McCown was the kind of guy who lived by the written rules, a bit naive, but always trying to be accepted. We concluded that Mac actually believed the story of the wheels up landing. And apparently, it worked for him."[13]

There was talk circulating in the various Marine squadrons of a "ghost" F4U that had been captured by the Japanese and flown against the Americans. Captain John M. Foster of VMF-222, recalls his strange encounter with a lone F4U on 15 February 1944. After leaving formation due to engine trouble, he spotted a single Corsair tailing him. He recalls: "I swung around into him and he turned into me, but he couldn't turn sharp enough. I was in a good position to boresight him, when I recognized the plane as an F4U."[14] Foster wheeled away and discovered that the Corsair was following him. Curious as to who the pilot could be, he slowed down to allow his friend to catch up. The mystery Corsair then turned around. Foster opened full throttle and tried to catch up, but the ghost plane was last seen heading toward Rabaul.

"Several weeks previously a pilot had been disabled by AA and crash-landed safely on Lakunai airfield without burning his plane," wrote Foster. "The pilot had always maintained he would rather land on the airstrip itself than bail out or land near Japanese ground forces. He thought the airfield personnel would treat him more decently."[15]

1. 253 Air Group mission report, 1 January 1944.
2. *Baa Baa Black Sheep*, 220-221. Boyington claimed six victories while flying with the American Volunteer Group ("Flying Tigers"), but only two claims could be verified through incomplete records, according to Frank Olynyk in USMC Credits for the Destruction of Enemy Aircraft in Air-To-Air Combat World War II, April 1982. On 3 January 1944, Boyington had 19 victories with the USMC and it was widely accepted that he had six additional victories with the AVG. After the war, his three additional claims on his last dogfight plus Ashmun's claim were officially accepted based on his word, a departure from Marine Corps policy. His official Marine Corps score is 22 aerial victories; his total unofficial score is 28. Most historians now consider Joe Foss to be the top Marine Corps ace with 26 victories.
3. Several former Zero pilots interviewed in Japan, including Sadamu Komachi and Takeo Tanimizu, indicated that it was extremely difficult to set an American fighter plane on fire. In a 1981 interview, Tanimizu remarked: "The only time you could really shoot down an F4U was when it was fleeing. You had to shoot at it from a certain angle (from the rear, from a higher position, into the cockpit area). Otherwise, the bullets would bounce off." He also noted: "You could always tell if it was a Zero or enemy plane that had crashed in the sea. The Zero left a fire on the surface, but the American plane just left an oil slick."
4. It was quite common for Japanese pilots to strafe Allied aviators in their parachutes or in the water. There were two reasons for this: In war, they believed that it was kill or be killed. Secondly, an enemy survivor will live to fight another day. A few Japanese pilots did not believe in killing a helpless opponent and spared them, but most did. Allied pilots who witnessed their comrades getting shot at in their parachutes retaliated in kind.
5. Telephone interview with Colonel Gregory Boyington, 1984.
6. Flight records of 204 and 253 Air Groups for 3 January 1944.
7. John M. Foster, *Hell in the Heavens*, Charter Books, New York, 1961, 234.
8. VMF-321 Aircraft Action Report, Report No.5, 4 January 1944.
9. Interview with Takeo Tanimizu, Osaka, Japan, 1979. Mr. Tanimizu told the author of this incident but could not determine the date. Ten years later while conducting research on his memoir, he was able to reconstruct the date. Carter's home was in Verdugo City, California, a small enclave in Glendale, but in 1992, a search for his next-of-kin, was unsuccessful. Mr. Tanimizu was saddened to learn that Carter was never rescued.
10. Correspondence with Major Leo Harmon, USMC (Ret.), 6 November 1991.
11. Correspondence with Robert Griffith, 1993.
12. Robert Brindos and about thirty other prisoners, in custody of the Japanese Army's 6th Field Kempei Tai (military police) were marched down Tunnel Hill Road toward Talili Bay in what is known as the "Tunnel Hill Incident." Major Saiji Matsuda, second in command of the Kempei Tai and in charge of the POW compound, still denies that the prisoners were executed. He stated that the captives were being moved to Watom Island for protection against Allied bombing. Bombers supposedly struck Talili where the prisoners were assembled, killing them all. Strangely, none of the Japanese guards were even wounded. Colonel Isamu Murayama, staff officer of the 17th Army in charge of Watom Island, never heard of the intended POW movement. General Hitoshi Imamura, commander of Rabaul's Army, stated that no orders were ever issued for such a move due to lack of shipping. Conveniently, all of the dead prisoners were cremated and buried on the spot. The Japanese stopped all cremations after February 1944 for fear of attracting Allied air attacks from smoke. They buried their own dead. It is difficult to believe that the Kempei Tai, who afforded the prisoners no medical attention nor very much food, would be concerned enough about their safety to move them to a safer location. Vague and conflicting war crimes statements by surviving Army and Navy officers and research by this author indicates that the thirty plus prisoners were executed in retaliation for the March 3rd bombing attack which totally destroyed downtown Rabaul.
13. Correspondence with Robert Griffith. McCown was never recovered.
14. *Hell in the Heavens*, 281.
15. Ibid. The author questioned former Japanese Navy Commander Tomoyoshi Hori about the possible capture of an F4U. His response in 1993: "I have never heard such a story. At the time, I had been around Lakunai Airfield as a staff officer of the 151st Air Group and used the airfield every day. If a F4U made such an emergency landing, I would have known about it. Thus, the mystery remains unsolved.

# 4

# PRISONERS OF WAR

Major Gregory "Pappy" Boyington was apprehensive and dazed as he was escorted ashore on Rabaul. Only hours before, he had been plucked from the sea by a Japanese submarine as he bobbed along in his one-man life raft. Blindfolded and tied, he was booted along the coral streets of downtown Rabaul by his captors until he came to a sudden stop.

"How would you like to be with your friends?" asked a voice in English without a trace of an accent. Blacksheep One was startled. After regaining his composure, Boyington responded: "I don't believe I know what you mean." Back came the smug reply: "Oh, you'll find out soon enough."[1]

"Soon enough" wasn't entirely soon enough for the disheveled Marine Corps major. The CO of VMF-214 was loaded onto a truck and taken to a building in town where he underwent his first interrogation.

"The Americanized voice I had heard before was there in front of me again," recalled Boyington. "I later

**Maj. Gregory "Pappy" Boyington, CO of VMF-214. (Credit: USMC)**

found out he was a boy who had gone as far as high school in Honolulu before his parents had sent him to Japan for further education."[2] Although the ex-Flying Tiger veteran would never learn the true identity of his new host, he and his fellow prisoners of war would eventually owe their lives to Edward Chikaki Honda.

Eddie Honda was born in 1911 in Ewa, Oahu (Territory of Hawaii) to Jiro and Mitsu Honda. His father Jiro worked for Oahu Railway Company as the superintendent of railway bridges. Young Eddie graduated from McKinley High School in 1929. His parents were devout Buddhists and sent their third son to Japan for a formal and religious education. The tall Hawaiian youngster excelled in baseball as a middle school student in Kyoto and decided to make the sport his profession.[3]

By 1938, "Chicky" Honda was a star outfielder for the reknowned Keio University Baseball Team. Despite the worsening war clouds looming on the horizon, the future looked bright. He secured a position as sportswriter for the prestigious Domei News Agency in 1939, but with a salary of only fifty yen a month, young Chikaki was constantly writing home for money. In 1941, the thirty year old transplanted Hawaiian married and became an assistant coach for the Nagoya Dragons Baseball Team.[4]

After many years in Japan, Honda was imbued with the Japanese spirit and voluntarily renounced his American citizenship in 1941. He joined the Navy as a civilian interpreter in 1942 and arrived in Rabaul in August 1943.

The Japanese Navy's method of interrogating English speaking prisoners was usually an exercise in futility. While many of the high ranking officers had studied English at the Naval Academy, very few understood the American and Allied lingos. Adding to the confusion was the wide variety of thick national and regional accents. Frustrated interrogators failed to understand Western psychology and values and resorted to torture, eliciting information of dubious value from the lips of injured and dying prisoners.

Chikaki Honda impressed his superiors with his ability to extract information from the captives. The savvy Hawaiian Nisei was a natural public relations man. Sympathetic words, delivered in the native lingo, with an ocassional gift of a cigarette, helped put the prisoners at ease. Much more personable than the stern-faced Japanese officers, one could not help but like the well meaning interpreter under the circumstances.

"Pappy" Boyington's initial interrogation was uncomforting to his ego and his physical well being. The Japanese officers unleashed a petty officer to beat the stubborn American. Unsatisfied with the answers, the interrogators snubbed out their cigarettes on the Marine's neck and shoulders.

When the officers left the room for a short break, Honda tendered some helpful advice to the battered Leatherneck. "Major Boyington, why don't you make it easy on yourself?" offered the concerned interpreter. "These 'Japs' are going to question you again and again on the same subjects. If you're going to give them a line, stick to the same story and be consistent; othewise, they will think you are lying and it will get very rough for you."[5]

"I came to like 'Suyako' in a very short time," recalled Boyington. "I took his advice. I couldn't argue with his logic. He understood my predicament."[6]

The shabby treatment of the blacksheep fighter ace by the Japanese would have delighted some of his Marine Corps superiors and shocked his comrades. Denied medical attention, his festering wounds and lack of hygiene made his mere presence offensive. Keeping a safe distance, the captors badgered him with a barrage of inane questions.

"Man, oh man, I was told many times by the interpreter, and by those who were interrogating me through the interpreter, that I was awfully stupid for a major," wrote Boyington. "And I felt at times like saying: 'What's more sport, there are those back at my base, who will agree with you, too.'"[7]

Lieutenant John M. Arbuckle, a PBY pilot of VP-52, who was shot down near Kavieng and captured in December 1943, recalls his interrogation in Rabaul:

"It took place at their headquarters which was built on stilts with no walls. The room was large and there were many people walking around, coming and going, and not paying any attention to me. My arms were untied and I sat in a chair. It was just me and the interpreter (Honda). He gave me cigarettes, hot tea, and these small red sour plums. The interpreter asked me many silly questions. One was 'Why was MacArthur called Dugout Doug?' and another was 'Is President Roosevelt really a Jew?' He was asking the questions from a list. We both knew that some of the questions were ridiculous and I would respond 'Ah, come on.' He'd shrug his shoulders and continue.

"He was really a likeable kid. He acted strict when he was with the officers. He never hit us, but did push us around, and it was all an act. When he was alone with us, he treated us nice and gave us advice. He never told me this real name, but he did say that he grew up in Hawaii and went to Japan to play professional baseball. He also said to me: 'I'm going to get out of Rabaul. You just wait and see!'"[8]

Unknown to Boyington and his group of prisoners, they were living on borrowed time. It was the policy

Edward "Chicky" Honda (left) and brother Ralph with wives in a postwar photo. (Credit: Ralph Honda)

of the Imperial Navy to execute their prisoners once information was wrung out of them. Tokyo had instructed Rabaul HQ not to send any more prisoners to the homeland.[9]

Little did the prisoners realize that "Suyako" had plans for them. The crafty Hawaiian knew the war situation through Allied radio transmissions and prisoner interrogations. It was only a matter of time before Rabaul was overrun. He convinced his superiors that Major Boyington and his comrades possessed valuable military information and should be sent to Tokyo for further interrogation. The ruse worked. Civilian Interpreter Chikaki Honda was ordered to escort the prisoners to Tokyo.[10]

1. *Baa Baa Blacksheep*, 234.
2. Ibid.
3. Biography of Edward Chikaki Honda, FAX transmission from Professor John J. Stephan, History Dept., University of Hawaii, 14 November 1995 and interview with Ralph Chikato Honda, Monterey, CA, 25 November 1995.
4. Ralph Honda interview.
5. Interview with Colonel Gregory Boyington, Fresno, CA, July 1987. "Suyako" was Boyington's mispronunciation of the Japanese word "tsuyaku" which means "interpreter."
6. Ibid.
7. *Baa Baa Blacksheep*, 243.
8. Telephone interview with John M. Arbuckle, 14 November 1995.
9. A study of documents from the Australian Archives pertaining to war crimes investigations at Rabaul revealed mass executions of Allied prisoners from 1942 until 1944. Allied military personnel captured by the Navy were under the custody of the Naval 81st Guards Unit which carried out executions while those captured by the Army were in the custody of the Army's 6th Field Kempei Tai (military police). No Allied prisoners emerged alive from Naval custody at the end of the war.
10. Arbuckle interview. He stated that his group of prisoners did not possess any information of military value. He is now convinced that Honda used them to get out of Rabaul.

22

# 5

# THE GREAT WITHDRAWAL

By February 1944 the Japanese had taken a tremendous beating at the hands of Allied Forces. Intense low level bombing of airfields had hampered their ability to fight back. However, their greatest losses were inflicted by American fighters; approximately ninety-six Zeroes were destroyed in January 1944 alone.[1]

The three main fighter groups at Rabaul were losing the war of attrition. On 3 January 1944, the 201st Air Group was ordered to withdraw to Saipan. The thirty surviving pilots packed their meager belongings and departed Rabaul, leaving behind their tired mounts. The once proud 204th had been whittled down to only one operational fighter by 17 February. The 253rd, temporarily aided by Zeroes from the 2nd Carrier Division, became Rabaul's last hope.

Most of the high scoring pilots were now history. Chief Petty Officer Takeo Okumura of the 201st, who reportedly scored over fifty victories, had been lost on 22 September 1943. Thirty-five Zeroes, escorting bombers on an attack against American convoy near Cape Cretin, New Guinea, were surprised by P-38s from

the 432nd Fighter Squadron and P-40s from the 35th Fighter Group. In a wild forty-five minute dogfight, Okumura disappeared. Just a week prior, he had received a coveted ceremonial sword from Admiral Kusaka for distinguished service.

Other notable pilots who became statistics included Chief Petty Officer Shizuo Ishii (204th Air Group), twenty-nine victories. Seventeen of his total score came in the last six weeks of his life. He was killed by Lightnings over Rabaul on 24 October 1943. Flight Seaman Hiroshi Shibagaki, another pace setter from the 204th, claimed all of his thirteen victories within two months after arriving at Rabaul. Marine Corsairs claimed him on 22 January 1944. Warrant Officer Nobuo Ogiya's eighteen victories in thirteen days set a military record. The 253rd veteran was killed on 13 February 1944 attacking SBDs and F4Us over Rabaul. His comrades say

Destined for Rabaul, the trainees and instructors (front row) of Hei 12 Class pose for their graduation photo. Hiroshi Shibagaki (third row from bottom, center) claimed 13 aircraft before he was killed. Masajiro Kawato is second from the right, top row. (Credit: Y. Izawa)

CPO Takeo Okumura in 1942. (Credit: Y. Izawa)

WO Nobuo Ogiya. (Credit: Y. Izawa)

he downed five on his last mission and died with twenty-four victories.

Empty sleeping places in the pilots' quarters were a stark reminder that even peerless skills were not enough to ensure survival. Depression and stress were evident.

Commander Masatake Okumiya, a staff air officer to the Second Air Fleet, had arrived at Rabaul on 20 January 1944. As soon as he walked into headquarters, he sensed something terribly wrong.

"Outwardly, the staff personnel were the same. Nevertheless they had changed. Six months ago they were cheerful, hard workers, despite the rigors of life at Buin. Now, they were quick-tempered and harsh, their faces grimly set. The fighting spirit which enabled us to ignore the worst of Buin was gone. The men lacked confidence; they appeared dull and apathetic. No longer were they the familiar well-functioning team."[2]

US Task Force 58 began steaming southwest from the Marshall Islands toward a group of coral atolls known as Truk, Japan's South Pacific "Gibraltar." The assault on Truk was a high priority target for Admiral Nimitz. Much more than a major Japanese Naval base,

Truk protected the Carolines and had to be neutralized. The enemy bastion could threaten projected American operations against the Marianas, the next island group to the north.[3]

An earlier photo reconnaissance flight by two Marine B-24s, led by Major James R. Christensen of Salt Lake City, detected the presence of two dozen large warships at Truk. When Admiral Nimitz heard the news, he was elated and decided to stage his own Pearl Harbor.[4] Admiral Spruance assumed overall tactical command of the operation and would engage the enemy in a surface action; Mitscher, the Naval aviation expert, would command the air strike from his flagship Yorktown. On the morning of 17 February 1944 they were in position to launch.

By a stroke of fate the great raid on Truk would be witnessed by six Allied prisoners of war. The captives had been brought together in the Naval prison at Rabaul on 15 February 1944. For Navy civilian interpreter Edward Chikaki Honda, these six prisoners were going to be his ticket out of the besieged base.

The group included Boyington, John M. Arbuckle, P-38 pilot Captain Charles Taylor, F4U pilot Major Don Boyle (VMF-212), one Aussie and a New Zealander. They boarded a Betty bomber on the morning of 17 February. All of the prisoners were blindfolded, handcuffed, and their legs bound. Besides the pilot and co-pilot, the only other Japanese on board were Honda, a guard, and the plane's rear gunner. Perhaps it was illusionary, but skyjacking was on Blacksheep One's mind.

"I also had the bonds on my hands so loose that I could have pulled my hands free in a second's notice," recalled Boyington. "But one of my six mates must have read my thoughts, or maybe he heard me mumble them, because he whispered: 'Greg, I pray you don't try to make an escape and take over this plane.'"[5]

Forty-six minutes before the end of their four hour flight, the Central Pacific offensive began with the launching of wave after wave of Grumman Hellcats of Task Force 58. Truk was about to be flattened.

The Betty bomber pilot had beaten Admiral Mitscher to Truk by seconds. The bone-jarring landing threw the passengers around like baggage. Recalled Boyington: "It happened to be the roughest, shortest of landings, intentionally I know now, I have ever experienced or ever hope to."[6] Hellcats screamed over the airfield spraying everything in sight.

"Hey, your carrier planes are attacking us!" yelled the interpreter. "We've got to get out of here and take cover!" He quickly went from prisoner to prisoner, untying their ankles and herding them toward the exit. The men stumbled forward and jumped out of the doomed bomber.[7]

"The piece of transportation we had just crawled out of went up before our eyes in flames and smoke, so did nearly every other plane we could see around here," observed Boyington. "It was one of the best Navy Day programs I ever expect to see, the first task-force raid on the island of Truk."[8]

The prisoners and Honda dived into a slit trench as the ground shook from thunderous explosions. An hour dragged by with no end in sight. The men seemed to be caught in the middle of the action. "You guys stay put right here!" ordered Honda. "I'm getting into a real foxhole!" The former baseball player bolted out of sight.

"Right after the interpreter ran off, about four or five Zero pilots jumped right on top of us!" recalls Arbuckle. "It was a funny, awkard situation. They were trying to get under cover. We really surprised them! They cursed us and one picked up some dirt and threw it at us."[9]

After the fireworks had died down in the afternoon, Honda came back to the pit. Surprisingly, all of the prisoners were alive. "Don't worry, they'll be angry, but I'll protect you," said Honda. This was reassuring to the helpless group. The Hawaiian-Japanese had now saved their lives twice.

The POWs eventually arrived in Japan via Saipan aboard a DC-3 transport plane. Boyington and his American comrades, and their benefactor, Edward Chikaki Honda, would all survive the war.[10]

The surprise raid on Truk failed to materialize into the Pearl Harbor scenario envisioned by Admiral Nimitz. Most of the Japanese men-of-war had departed before the onslaught, and the Commander-in-Chief of the Pacific Fleet had to settle for mostly merchant ships with a handful of cruisers and destroyers. However, Fifth Fleet aviators claimed 127 enemy aircraft destroyed in the air and another seventy-seven destroyed on the ground.[11]

When nine carriers of US Task Force 58 had finished with Truk, Admiral Mineichi Koga, head of the Combined Fleet, ordered an immediate reinforcement of aircraft. Almost all of his inventory were destroyed during the two day rampage. The desperate situation on Truk forced him to request a quick loan of aircraft from Rabaul. With the war situation deteriorating, Admiral Kusaka realized that his boss was not a good credit risk, but he couldn't refuse.

Admiral Halsey decided it was time to hurl an insult at Rabaul, ordering five destroyers of DesRon 12 (*Farenholt, Buchanan, Landsdowne, Lardner,* and *Woodworth*) to conduct a bombardment of Simpson Harbor on the night of 18/19 February. The destroyers, in column formation, shelled various targets with almost 4,000 rounds of five-inch projectiles and fifteen torpedoes were fired into Keravia Bay.[12]

The audacity of the American attack by surface ships infuriated the Japanese. The brazen Yanks continued to hurl their shells with wild abandon while the defenders crouched low in their underground shelters cursing the Americans. Rabaul's thirty-eight coastal guns remained eerily silent. The cannons had been installed for short distance firing to counter any landing attempts. Coast defense was primarily the Navy's responsibility and their inability to counter the enemy's assault was humiliating.

Chief Petty Officer Sadamu Komachi was livid with anger and disgusted that Rabaul could mount no response. He told his bewildered commanders that he would attack the enemy destroyers himself. Despite the hazards of night flying, they raised no objections. The Navy's integrity had to be salvaged.

Komachi took off from Tobera with two 60-kg bombs strapped under the wings. Purple flashes on the horizon pinpointed the location of the destroyers. They were now off the coast of Kokopo. The Zero pilot could see fires burning along the coast. In the darkness, he could see the white wakes and faint forms of the vessels as they cut silently through the waters.

The lone Zero dove with guns blazing. Komachi was in danger of plunging into the sea as it is extremely difficult to gauge altitude in the dark. Surprisingly no searchlights came on. The Zero climbed to 3,000 feet and dove again for the attack. Aiming at the second destroyer in the formation, two bombs were released. When the bombs detonated off target, the destroyers' anti-aircraft response was immediate and fierce. They turned their stems in unison and fled toward the open sea.

On *Lardner*, engineering officer Lieutenant (j.g.) Edward R. Brown was ordered to generate smoke to confuse the enemy pilot. Gunners sent up a wall of flak and machine gun fire but Komachi maneuvered out of range, then came back for another strafing run. He noticed fires burning on the ships and repeated his attacks until his ammunition supply was exhausted. Satisfied with his handiwork, Komachi headed home.

"I attacked the destroyers and set small to medium fires on three of them!" reported Komachi to his commanders. "I chased them out of the bay." The twenty-three year old six-foot daredevil had saved the Navy's face.[13]

On the destroyers, the crewmen surveyed the "damage." In their haste to fire back, the gunners had simply fired through the gun covers, setting them on fire! Edward Brown, now an attorney in Encino, California, described the damage: "The gun barrels were very hot. Hence the damage control party had to continously wet them down, as the bloomers on the five-inch battery caught on fire."[14]

Fifth Air Force B-25s again attacked shipping in Simpson Harbor on 19 February 1944. Lieutenant Commander Tommy Blackburn and his "Jolly Rogers" prowled the sky on escort duty. Along with SBDs and TBF bombers, they were picked up by Cape St. George radar, and the warning reached Tobera Airfield. Chief Petty Officer Tetsuzo Iwamoto led twenty-six Zeroes into the air to greet the Americans.

Basil Henning, CO Tom Blackburn and Ira Kepford celebrate on 19 Feb 44, when VF-17 completed their combat tour after a 16 victory day. Their final score was 154 . (Credit: Tom Blackburn)

While Blackburn and his Corsairs were riding herd on the slow moving bombers, he ordered Lieutenant (j.g.) Danny Cunningham and Lieutenant Oscar Chenoweth to scout ahead. The pair of Corsairs arrived high over Cape St. George at 30,000 feet. Six to eight Zeroes were spotted below at 18,000 and the two Pirates dove to attack. The Japanese scattered like pigeons, but Chenoweth latched onto one Zero and sent him crashing. Through fine team work, they kept the Japanese off their backs and scored. Cunningham, who had three victories before entering the morning's melee, became an ace when he claimed four more to up his score to seven. Chenoweth added three more to push his tally to eight and one-half.

Initially Blackburn observed that the Zeroes weren't very aggressive. However, Japanese tactics changed during retirement of the strike force. Iwamoto noted in his diary:

"Our fighters were already engaged with the escort fighters. The bomber group was now trying to retreat. This was the opportunity we had been waiting for. We dove from 9,000 meters; the main force attacked the bombers while a few of us attacked the F4Us above."[15]

The 253rd pilots concentrated their attention on the slower SBDs. Iwamoto believed that they downed ten of them in five minutes. The Corsairs proved too much to handle and orders were given to withdraw and regroup. After a brief respite, the Japanese were back again, slugging it out with the F4Us. In the meantime, the bombers rendered Tobera Airfield inoperable. The returning Zeroes were forced to land at Vunakanau.

Despite all the victory claims, the 253rd had lost only five aircraft. Their pilots claimed thirty-seven enemy aircraft shot down with six probables. The "Jolly Rogers" came out without a scratch, and with sixteen claimed victories, finished their first tour of duty with a record 154 victories in seventy-six days.[16] VF-38 pilots claimed five victories, one probable, and four damaged and suffered no losses. The Marines missed out on the carnage and VMF-222 lost one Corsair but its pilot was saved. There were no TBF losses, but VMSB-244 did loose one SBD to an unknown cause.

An exhausted Chief Petty Officer Iwamoto finally came back to base after dark. He had landed at another airfield and waited until part of Tobera's runway had been patched. After a brief rest, he was called into a secret conference at air group headquarters. Commander Taro Fukuda looked solemnly at Iwamoto, Lieutenants Tatsuo Hirano and Shiroshita, and the chief of the ground crews. Then he gave the chilling news: catastrophic death and destruction at Truk by American carrier planes. Fukuda had been given his marching orders that afternoon from the Eleventh Air Fleet. He warned his subordinates to keep this a secret for now and prepare for immediate withdrawal.[17]

1. *U.S.S.B.S.*, 50.
2. *Zero!,*Masatake Okumiya and Jiro Horikoshi, with Martin Caidin, Ballantine Books, New York, 1979, 222-223.
3. Lieutenant Oliver Jensen, USNR, *Carrier War*, Pocket Books, New York, 1945, 97.
4. Ibid.
5. *Baa Baa Blacksheep*, 248. John M. Arbuckle questions Boyington's recollection and says "I think he was exaggerating. Our arms, wrists, and feet were bound and we were blindfolded and gagged. We couldn't talk to each other!"
6. Ibid., 249.
7. Telephone interview with John M. Arbuckle, 5 December 1995.
8. *Baa Baa Blacksheep*, 249.
9. Arbuckle interview.
10. Edward C. Honda was arrrested by the US Army Counter Intelligence Corps in Japan after the war. He had met some old friends who were serving in the Occupation Force and they told

With yet another form of abuse, the 500th Bomb Sq. delivers a phosphorous bomb attack on Rabual's anti-aircraft gun batteries 2 Nov. 43. (Credit: J.C. Hanna)

Vice Adm. Kusaka (in dark cap) patiently awaits the return of his dwindling air force from a mission. A capable leader, he headed the Japanese Naval Academy at Etajima before his assignment to Rabaul. (Credit: Maru)

him that the CIC was looking for him. He turned himself in. During the interview, they noticed a watch that Boyington had given him. He was arrested on the charge of stealing the watch and also for being the head of the Civilian Intelligence Corps utilizing Niseis. Honda was transported to Guam for war crimes trial. When contacted, Boyington responded: "Yes, I gave him the watch. It was broken, so I had no more use for it, and told him he could fix it up and keep it. He is a good gent, treat him right, and please wish him the Season's Greetings, most sincerely, for me." The theft charge was dismissed. When it was confirmed that Honda had renounced his American citizenship in 1941, he could not be tried for treason. He spent six months on Guam, having the time of his life playing baseball and enjoying the amenties of the military PX. Edward Chikaki Honda became a public relations consultant and was active in postwar baseball. He died in 1989 in Japan. Colonel Gregory Boyington died on 11 January 1988 at age 75 and is buried in Arlington National Cemetary. He was contemptuos of his Medal of Honor because he felt he did not deserve it; he believed the Marine Corps used him to enhance the Corps' image. When asked in later years to show his award, he remarked that he kept it in a coffee can in his garage where it had become rusty. Don Boyle is still alive and John M. Arbuckle is a retired professor of Naval science residing in Texas.

11. *Carrier War*, 102.
12. Theodore Roscoe, *United States Destroyer Operations in World War II*, US Naval Institute, 1953, 272.
13. Interview with Sadamu Komachi, Tokyo, Japan, 1981. Komachi is alive and well in Tokyo. In 1992, he was a guest of the Naval Aviation Museum Foundation and visited Pensacola, Florida to be a panelist in the Battle of Coral Sea Symposium. "I'm just a lowly warrant officer, but I had admirals and captains saluting me and shaking my hand. This would never happen in Japan!" he remarked.
14. Correspondence from Edward R. Brown, 5 November 1984.
15. *Zero-Sen Gekitsui O.*
16. *The Jolly Rogers*, viii.
17. *Zero-Sen Gekitsui O.*

# 6

# REBIRTH OF A ZERO SQUADRON

Vice Admiral Jin-Ichi Kusaka, commander of the Eleventh Air Fleet, knew the importance of air defense for Rabaul. The thunderous assault on Truk by American carrier aircraft and Admiral Koga's immediate request for all of Rabaul's airworthy aircraft stunned him. Admiral Koga had assured him that the Zeroes would eventually be returned.

Kusaka arrived at Lakunai Airfield on 20 February 1944 with his staff to watch the departure. Turning to Captain Takeshi Sanagi and Commander Tomoyoshi Hori, he sighed in despair, "They're never coming back. Never! But it can't be helped. We'll just have to do the best we can with what we have." He felt certain that Tokyo had abandoned Rabaul to its fate.[1]

The orderly departure of aircraft, pilots, and support personnel began on the 20th and didn't end until 24-25 February. About thirty Zeroes, six Betty bombers, eight Val dive bombers, ten Judy single-engine bombers, and five or six Kate torpedo planes departed for Truk.[2]

The exodus also caught the attention of some Allied prisoners of war languishing in the Japanese Army's 6th Field Kempei Tai (military police) prison in downtown Rabaul. Second Lieutenant Jose Holguin (65th Bomb Squadron, USAAF) looked up and remembered: "For about one or two hours that morning, airplanes took off from the various airfields around Rabaul and circled and formed over the harbor. It was quite a sight, but we were surprised that there were that many airplanes still left on Rabaul, considering the incessant bombings of the past few months. We counted about thirty fighters and fifteen bombers."[3]

What Admiral Kusaka had left behind were fifteen grounded Zero fighters in various stages of disrepair. Orders were given to make them operational.[4] A few veterans and about thirty inexperienced (and mostly sick and disabled) Zero pilots from the various squadrons were also left at Rabaul.[5] These weary aircraft and tired pilots were a sad reminder of better days and a mockery to Admiral Kusaka.

Admiral Kusaka's inventory of patrol aircraft were equally dismal. The 151st Air Group, which shared Lakunai Airfield with the Army Air Force, now had one Type 100 Reconnaissance plane (Dinah) which was appropriated from the Army. There were four twin-engine Nakajima *Gekko* nightfighters (Irvings) out of commission, a handful of transport planes (converted bombers) and also a few Mavis flying boats.

Rabaul's other partner in the guardian angel business was the 958th Air Group. The 958th was a seaplane reconnaissance unit which arrived at Rabaul in April 1942. It was originally equipped with the twin-float Jakes and single-float Pete biplanes.

The Jake was the Navy's Type O Observation Seaplane, manufactured by Aichi under the designation E13A. Designed in 1937, it made its first combat debut in late 1941 over the China coast. It carried a crew of three and could cruise for over 15 hours, making it one of the most successful Japanese reconnaissance planes ever built.

The Pete, designated F1M, was the Navy's single-float biplane scout. Remarkably, this aircraft was well adapted for reconnaissance, patrol, dive-bombing, and fighter interception. It was armed with two 7.7mm machine guns in the nose and a single gun in the rear observer's position. Despite its obsolete appearance, this biplane was the most widely manufactured of all single-engine reconnaissance aircraft in the Navy's arsenal.

At the end of February 1944, all of the Petes were transferred to Truk, leaving the 958th with just eight Jakes and a dozen pilots. The unit operated independently of the fighter squadron and was under the control of Rabaul HQ.

Most of the aviation forces, including anti-aircraft units remaining behind, were organized into infantry, and prepared to defend against the assumed invasion. Emphasis was placed on demolition training against tanks, utilizing bombs and mines. They also received extensive training against enemy parachute landings.[6]

Rabaul's "Guerrilla Air Force" came into being with the hasty departure of the 253rd. The only hardcore veterans of this ersatz unit were Warrant Officer Shigeo Fukumoto, Chief Petty Officer Tokushige Yoshizawa, and Petty Officer Sekizen Shibayama.

Shigeo Fukumoto, age 23, was an old hand in the 253rd and was well liked. "He wasn't overly strict and he was someone you could talk to," said a subordinate.[7] He had joined the Navy in 1936 and was regarded by a comrade as, "an excellent veteran pilot equivalent to Saburo Sakai."[8] (Sakai had scored over 60 enemy planes destroyed or damaged and was one of the Navy's top pilots). Indicative of Fukumoto's skill was the 72 victories he would claim at the end of the war.

Tokushige Yoshizawa, 20, had nine victories to his credit and a wealth of experience. He had enlisted in 1940 and completed flight training in March 1943. Initially posted to the 201st Air Group at Buin (Bougainville Island), Yoshizawa transferred to Rabaul and served with the 204th. He was flying daily combat missions over Rabaul until malaria grounded him.

Sekizen Shibayama, 21, had arrived at Rabaul in September 1943 and flew with the 201st Air Group. Prior to his arrival, he had worked as a flight instructor for five months at Yatabe Air Base in the homeland.

On 11 November 1943, Shibayama took his brand new Zero up to defend Lakunai Airfield. Climbing over the enemy's top cover, the Zero's engine began running rough as he dove to attack. He found himself in the midst of eight Hellcats as his aircraft came sputtering out of the clouds. While the unwelcome party crasher studied his gauges, Lieutenant Armistead "Chick" Smith Jr. of VF-9 clobbered him. A .50 caliber slug missed Shibayama's "crown jewels" by inches.

Shibayama glided his Zero into the water. Upon contact, the aircraft flipped over on its back, but the pilot successfully extricated himself. For the next two hours, the young pilot watched the combat overhead until rescued by a picket boat. A case of malaria and a leg injury had prevented his departure from Rabaul.[9]

The remaining pilots were relative neophytes. Although lacking much combat experience, they were a spirited group of youngsters. Entrusted with the air defense of Rabaul, they took their assignments seriously.

**PO Yasushi Shimbo at Tobera. (Credit: Y. Kanai)**

Chief Petty Officer Yasushi Shimbo was a good pilot who had entered the Navy in January 1941. He did his flight training at Tsuchiura, one of the Navy's top flight schools. His flight schooling amounted to 190 hours on trainers before converting to Zeroes. He had only forty hours of operational training in the Zero. Prior to his arrival at Rabaul in December 1943, he underwent brief combat training with the Atsugi Air Group.[10]

Shimbo flew his first mission at Rabaul on 7 January 1944. On his second mission (9 January), he engaged F4Us of VMF-321 over Tobera Airfield. The Americans sent in TBF bombers to hole Tobera Airfield, escorted by Marine F4Us, Navy F6Fs, and RNZAF P-40s.

According to the VMF-321 mission report:

"Lt. See and wingman, Capt. McCown, covered the TBF's over the target, circling, while they bombed. They dropped down on three Zekes, coming in from six o'clock with a slight altitude advantage. See opened up at about 250 yards. With one long burst, he kept firing until passing over the enemy aircraft. There was a small explosion, possibly a wing tank. The Zeke went down bellowing black smoke."[11]

Lieutenant See's victim was Shimbo, who was hit in the wing tank. He landed his smoking aircraft and escaped unharmed.

Shimbo later went back into combat and claimed three Allied fighters shot down (a P-38 on 14 or 15 January, and two Corsairs on 24 or 25 January 1944). By 7 February he had flown an incredible eighteen combat missions. Because he had sustained an arm injury he was one of those left behind.

Petty Officer Fumio Wako entered combat over Rabaul on 7 January 1944. He was hit by a Corsair in February and parachuted down with burns. Unfit to fly, he was grounded and missed the withdrawal.[12]

Petty Officer Yoshinobu Ikeda received his flight training at Iwakuni Airfield near Hiroshima and was posted to the 281st Air Group. He was sent to Northern Japan (Kurile Islands) where he fought the elements, but saw no combat. When it started snowing heavily, his unit was sent packing to the Marshall Islands where they saw immediate action. He tangled with three P-39s of the 72nd Squadron on 19 December 1943 over Mili Atoll and claimed one shot down, but he received minor wounds to his left arm when his plane was struck by an explosive shell. "If I had been shot down into the sea, I would have wound up as shark bait!" he recalls. "And whenever I see ducks flying, they remind me of the Bell P-39!"[13]

Petty Officers Yoshinobu Ikeda and his comrade, Gensaku Aoki, arrived at Rabaul from the Marshall Islands on 9 January. Ikeda entered combat on 12 January, followed by Aoki three days later.

On 18 February 1944, two days before the great withdrawal to Truk, there was a raid over Tobera Airfield by P-38s of the 339th Fighter Squadron. Petty Of-

A photo for the newspaper back home taken at Rabaul early 1944. L. to R. Takashi Kaneko, Masajiro Kawato, an unknown Asahi reporter and Yoshinobu Ikeda. (Credit: Y. Ikeda)

ficer Ikeda's Zero had a bad engine, so he quickly changed mounts and roared off, trying to catch up with his comrades. However, the canopy had not been cleaned; dirt and grime obscured his vision. As he was climbing to 1,500 feet over the strip, his Zero was hit from behind.

Gas vapor spewed into the cockpit from under Ikeda's seat. Hot oil spurted out from around his foot pedal like a geyser. Luckily, there was no fire but panic gripped him. The engine began to loose power and the aircraft gradually lost altitude. A parachute exit was out of the question; he was too low for a safe bail out. He plowed into a coconut grove near Keravat Airfield totaling both his aircraft and a tree.[14]

Ikeda suffered an injury to his right eye, a cut upper lip, and shock. Without his aircraft, he was doomed to stay at Rabaul. As for his squadronmate, Gensaku Aoki, there wasn't a Zero for him to fly out either, so he also missed the exodus.

Flight Seaman Third Class Masajiro Kawato was a baby-faced eighteen year old who desperately wanted to prove himself. He had joined the 253rd on 10 October 1943, fresh from Japan. Shortly after his arrival, during a squadron lineup, an officer humiliated him in front of Commander Taro Fukuda (air group commander) and the entire squadron. "I wonder if a child like you can fight in this war?" asked a sarcastic officer in a loud voice.[15] Kawato was infuriated and vowed to make a name for himself.

Kawato's first brush with death had occurred on 11 November 1943 when the US Fifth Air Force teamed up with the Navy to launched its last great raid against Rabaul. B-24s softened up Lakunai Airfield without interference. Carrier Task Groups 50.3 and 50.4 (*Essex*, *Bunker Hill*, *Independence*, *Saratoga* and *Princeton* launched a total of 125 bombers (SBDs, TBFs, and SB2Cs) to attack shipping in Simpson Harbor. To add to the spectacle, they also dispatched 127 F6F Hellcats.

PO Gensaku Aoki at Tateyama Air Base in Japan. (Credit: G. Aoki)

Kawato was blasted from the sky over Simpson Harbor, most likely by VF-9 Hellcats, bailed out and swam ashore. Total American losses that day were six TBFs and eight Hellcats; the Japanese lost eleven Zeroes.

If there was a guardian angel, Kawato had one. On 17 December 1943, during the first single-engine fighter sweep over Rabaul by Allied land-based fighters, Kawato collided with a New Zealand P-40 flown by Flight Lieutenant John O. McFarlane of 16 Squadron. The Kiwi made a head-on attack against Kawato, but the feisty teenager refused to be intimidated. In a dangerous game of "chicken," the Kittyhawk and the Zero connected with their left wings. Kawato was thrown out of his plane by the violent impact, blacking him out.[16] Luckily, his parachute deployed, thanks to the static line which he had connected to his seat.

McFarlane's plane was last seen diving vertically into the bay behind Mt. Turanguna. Both pilots landed in the water near each other. The injured New Zealander swam toward his opponent, pistol in hand. Kawato shouted and gestured to McFarlane to throw his weapon away. Finally realizing that he would soon be captured, he tossed it. The two pilots were picked up shortly by a high speed boat. McFarlane had suf-

fered a gash on his head. Both shared a laugh over their unfortunate meeting while receiving medical treatment.[17]

According to Kawato, Flight Lieutenant McFarlane was shipped to Japan. His ultimate fate is unknown, but he was most likely executed at Rabaul. Royal New Zealand Air Force records state: "His death has since been presumed to have occurred on 17 December 1943."[18] He had just turned twenty-three the day before.

Kawato had another bad day on 6 February 1944 when he was shot down over Simpson Harbor by a fighter. This marked his thirty-fifth mission since 1 December 1943 and his third loss of a Zero. He parachuted into the harbor and swam ashore. Disabled with a leg wound and unfit to fly, Kawato was ordered to remain behind.

Work began immediately to repair the junk fleet of Zeroes. A bombing raid on Tobera Airfield in late February wiped out eight of the precious fighters. Captain Yoshio Yamakawa, commanding the 108th Aircraft Repair Shop, was called upon to resurrect the dead air squadron.

Mechanics labored day and night, rebuilding engines and dissecting bomb-damaged Zero fighters strewn about in the rubber forests. Lieutenant Yoshiku Kitagawa remembers the difficulties and frustration:

"Under orders, we dug a cave ten meters wide, three meters high, and fifty meters long. We stocked it with all sorts of parts and machine tools necessary to establish a remanufacturing workshop. Initially, we began to rebuild two Zeroes. The remains of the fuselage and wings were bent and twisted by bombing. There were so many holes in many of the parts that we simply couldn't use them."[19]

The machine shop facility was located in the forest of Ririe on the coast of Keravia Bay. Machine tools and engineers were transferred there to manufacture aircraft parts. Aircraft were assembled under the trees in the forests near Lakunai, Vunakanau, and Tobera Airfields.

By 28 February 1944, the 108th had completely overhauled six fighters, and the 253rd Air Group was back in the war. All six fighters were sent aloft on a formation training exercise where they encountered a New Zealand PV-1 of 2 BR Squadron. The pilot of the twin-engaged Ventura was Squadron Leader L.A.B. Greenaway who had been on a reconnaissance mission to New Britain. The squadron report stated: "Six enemy fighters were encountered near Mope Village, but only one made a serious attack and it was driven off by F/L A.T. Rowe, S/L Greenaway's turret gunner."[21]

At the beginning of March, Rabaul received two additional "new" Zero fighters. The pair of mongrelized aircraft would have embarrassed Mitsubishi, but they

This small foundry, essential to the rebuilding of Rabaul's derilict aircraft, was carefully hidden under dense jungle growth. Great care was taken to prevent excessive escape of smoke which invited air attacks. (Credit: H. Sakaida)

One of Rabaul's many damaged and cannibalized Mitsubishi Zero fighters, this one being examined by two Aussies at Lakunai Airfield after the surrender. (Credit: RNZAF)

were functional and a source of great pride to the engineers and mechanics of Yamakawa's unit.

Unknown to the Japanese, Allied Forces had decided to bypass Rabaul. With the capture of Lae and Salamaua in New Guinea, Cape Gloucester on the western end of New Britain Island, and seizure of the Admiralty Islands, Rabaul had lost its importance. Now completely cut off, it no longer contributed to the defense of the Japanese Empire. The defenders, however, were convinced that invasion was imminent.

1. Interview with Tomoyoshi Hori, 20 October 1993, Temple City, CA.
2. *U.S.S.B.S.*, 47-48.
3. Private memoir of Jose L. Holguin, 1988.
4. Squadron Leader D.S. Hamilton (RNZAF), Interrogation of Japanese Aircrew, Appendix to Report, via David J. Duxbury. There has been much confusion as to the number of Zero aircraft left on Rabaul. According to Ikuhiko Hata and Yasuho Izawa, there were nine. Commander Hori, in a correspondence dated 1 March 1993, confirmed the figure of 15 Zeroes by Hamilton.
5. Correspondence from Tomoyoshi Hori, 1 March 1993.
6. *U.S.S.B.S.*, 49.
7. Correspondence from Yoshinobu Ikeda, 28 March 1994.
8. Correspondence from Sekizen Shibayama, 1993.
9. Ibid.
10. Interrogation of Japanese Aircrew.
11. VMF-321 Aircraft Action Report, Report No.9, 9 January 1944.
12. Correspondence from Fumio Wako, 6 January 1992. His name could be pronounced Wakao in written Japanese, but in his letter to me, he wrote Wako in English.
13. Ikeda correspondence.
14. Ibid, 10 February 1992.
15. Masajiro Kawato, *Zero-Sen Rabaul Ni Ari* (Zero Fighters Exist At Rabaul), Konnichi No Wadai Publishers, Tokyo, Japan, 1956.
16. Ibid.
17. Ibid.
18. Biography of F/L John O. McFarlane supplied by Headquarters New Zealand Defence Force, 1986.
19. Yoshiku Kitagawa, quoted in Maru Magazine article "Rabaul's Last Zero Squadron," Kojinsha Publishers, Tokyo, Japan, 1975.
20. Correspondence from Tomoyoshi Hori, 4 May 1994.
21. No. 2 BR Squadron RNZAF Operations Record Book for 28 January 1944, via David J. Duxbury in his correspondence of 12 February 1992.

# 7

# DOGFIGHTS OVER TOBERA

Warrant Officer Shigeo Fukumoto needed to quickly whip his mixture of veterans and neophyte pilots into team players. The odd mixture of seven pilots flying seven decrepit aircraft in the face of overwhelming Allied air superiority had to give the impression that Rabaul still had airpower.

Aerial photographs of Rabaul by American aircraft on 25 February 1944 showed thirty-three grounded aircraft.[1] Most of these planes were hulks or decoys, those under restoration carefully hidden under trees. Of Rabaul's four major airstrips, Tobera had the shortest runway, a concrete strip 3,600 feet long and one hundred wide. This dismayed the Zero pilots who were used to longer runs. Fukumoto placed emphasis on formation flying, dive bombing, take-off and landing.

The Allies continued to fly combat air patrols to Rabaul and the Japanese noted that the enemy fighters went over at very fixed schedules. They quickly devised a "cat and mouse" game by training at dusk or very early in the morning.[2] This tranquillity was to change one day when there was an inadvertent scheduling error.

On 3 March 1944, the Japanese had their first encounter with the Americans. At 1620, seven Zeroes led by Warrant Officer Shigeo Fukumoto took off from Tobera. They were assembling over the airfield at 6,000 feet when they were spotted by Major Robert P. Keller, the commanding officer of VMF-223. The Marines in their

**WO Shigeo Fukumoto with the 302nd Air Group at Atsugi, Japan, in 1945. (Credit: K. Osuo)**

Corsairs were leading Navy Hellcats on a special reconnaissance mission to Rabaul to determine if the enemy plane strength was being increased.

"Joe Angyal and Archie Hunter flew my wings - the Navy F6Fs followed," recalled Keller. "We arrived over Simpson Harbor somewhere close to four PM, spotted perhaps eight Japanese fighters well below and dove to the attack. I fired my six .50 caliber guns into their leader; he burst into flames and I pulled up and away. I then discovered that both Angyal and Hunter had disappeared. I turned back toward the area of engagement and spotted a parachute which I assumed to be covering the pilot of my aircraft kill.

"I then spotted the other Japanese below me and dove to attack them. They split and I followed one, firing at but not seriously damaging him before I broke off the attack. The reason I broke off from him was that I heard an American pilot say, 'There's a whole bunch of them here.' I reasoned that my tail was vulnerable without a wingman and since there were apparently quite a number of enemy aircraft in the vicinity, I had best try to reform my three-man flight, which I was able to do through radio communication. We returned to Torokina with no further action. We had no losses nor am I aware of any other U.S. losses that day."[3]

Major Keller was credited with one Zero destroyed and another damaged; Lieutenant Joseph Angyal Jr. was credited with a probable. The three Corsairs returned to their base at 1900 hours.

The Japanese version of this encounter tells quite another story. According to official records, they lost no fighters and claimed five victories! Major General Bob Keller (retired), now residing in Pensacola, Florida, comments: "Perhaps the Japanese were talking about another time or place, or maybe their historian consumed too heavy a load of sake!"[4]

The Zero pilots had another close call three days later on 6 March. The war diary of VMF-217 records the following close encounter:

"This morning twelve of our planes escorted B-25s to Tobera. The escort planes were led by division leaders, Major J.M. Miller, Major T. Wojcik and Capt. J.D. Hench. As the flight passed over Rapopo, 1st Lt. M.R. Jones saw seven brown Jap aircraft in the traffic circle above the field. Lt. Jones approached the enemy aircraft from the rear and was about to fire when light A.A. fire arose from the field. The enemy aircraft instantly dispersed and Lt. Jones was not able to attack. Four of the Japs reversed their direction and maneuvered to a position on his tail and he was forced to use water injection to escape."[5]

It was only a matter of time before the Marines and the Japanese would clash again. Seven Zeroes, led by Petty Officer Sekizen Shibayama, took off just before noon on 12 March. It was another routine training flight consisting of Yasushi Shimbo, Masajiro Kawato, Fumio Wako, Kentaro Miyagoshi, Munetoshi Harada, and Etsuo Okimura. They climbed to 2,000 feet and began circling the airfield. In another case of bad timing, the Japanese were spotted by pilots of VMF-222. The "Flying Deuces" had participated in the first fighter sweep over Rabaul on 17 December 1943. This mission would mark the last major dogfight between the Japanese and the Marines over Rabaul.

Captain Henry M. Turner was in the lead, skimming over to Tobera at tree-top level. Another flight of Corsairs, led by Major Donald H. Sapp, the twenty-eight year old squadron executive officer, was coming in over St. George's Channel. He already was an ace with eight victories under his belt. Calling himself "Slap Happy Sappy the Mental Midget," he was regarded as the best pilot in his squadron with uncanny marksmanship and luck.

Anxious to make up for the lack of recent action, the Marines charged into the four Zeroes, but three other Japanese waiting several hundred feet above came screaming down with their guns blazing. The startled Leathernecks, saved by their opponents' poor

gunnery, used full power to outrun the Zeroes, pulled up to 6,000 feet, made a U-turn in a convenient cumulous cloud and raced after the attackers. The Japanese, badly outnumbered, tried to entice the Americans to come down to low altitude by circling the airfield at 300 feet. It was another trap. Anti-aircraft batteries surrounding the airfield waited to catch the Corsairs in a lethal crossfire.

Major Sapp understood what was happening but dove at the enemy regardless of the flak potential. The ground gunners opened up with a tremendous barrage. Captain Robert W. Wilson accompanied Sapp. The Zeroes were in a group of three, with one "Tail-end Charlie" lagging behind, and Sapp set his sights on the trailer.

The two Corsairs raced through the deadly bursts of flak. Sapp gave his victim a two second burst that reportedly blew the Zero out of the sky. He then slid over and fired on another Zero, which smoked and fell off in a diving turn from 250 feet. He didn't have time to watch it crash. Sapp immediately hammered at another Zero and saw pieces fly from the right wing. As they reached the end of the airstrip, the Zero tightened its turn and Sapp had too much speed for efficient lead, so the enemy aircraft got away.

Robert Wilson had picked out a Zero flown by Petty Officer Munetoshi Harada. A three-second burst from 150 yards proved fatal. The aircraft started to burn and hit in the revetment area at the southeast end of the strip.

As the two victorious Marines climbed toward Kabanga Bay for a brief respite they observed two more Zeroes in a traffic pattern preparing to land. Without a word, Sapp wrenched his plane around, losing Wilson in the process and dove through intense ground fire and caught a Zero with its wheels down with barely fifty

The Flying Deuces, VMF-222 pose on Espiritu Santo in Sept 1943. (L. to R.) Front row: George C. Schaefer, Don Sapp, CO Max Volcansek, Jr., Al Gordon, Pierre Carnagey and John Brittingham. Second row: William Carrell, James Williams III, Jesse Leach Jr., Robert Wilson, John Morris, Winfred Reid, John Foster. Third row: John Witt, John Nugent, Richard Hobbs, Henry Turner, Joe Craig III, Carl McLean, Wesley Hazlett, Robert Schaefer. Back row: Paul Parkhurst, John Newlands, Fred Hughes, Charles Jones, Wayne Gher, Stephen Yeager, Julius Koetsch and Irwin Moore. (Credit: National Archives)

feet of altitude. Petty Officer Etsuo Okimura, completely off guard, didn't have a chance. He was hit and crashed into the jungle northwest of the strip.

Official Japanese records acknowledge two Zeroes lost on 12 March 1944. They reported that seven Zeroes fought over fifty enemy aircraft and shot down two! Fumio Wako, who participated in this action, writes: "We had just left the airfield a few minutes before the Americans arrived. We were at low altitude and lost two aircraft."[6]

American records gave Major Sapp credit for two Zeroes shot down, a probable, and a damaged. Sapp ended the war with ten victories. He changed his name to Stapp after the war and passed away in 1989.

Captain Robert W. Wilson received credit for one destroyed and remembers this combat well.

"We had been going to Rabaul for some time without being challenged, so on that day it came as a surprise to see enemy fighters. My most vivid memory is seeing the bullets hit the airplane, seeing it burn and then actually crash, because the action took place at very low altitude right over the field. At the time those actions seemed very impersonal - it was man (me) against a machine (him). But when you put the name of the Japanese as Harada, it makes it so human. Having lived in Japan and met so many fine young men there, it all seems so pointless."[7]

Wilson ended the war with three victories and commanded Marine Air Group 33 at El Toro, California in 1964; the retired colonel is now an avocado rancher in Fallbrook, California.

As this combat was nearing its end, Zeroes scattered from the Tobera area and tried to regroup over Ataliklikun Bay, northeast of Vunakanau, but bad luck was the order of their day. Major Benjamin S. Hargrave Jr., commanding officer of VMF-216 leading two divisions (eight F4Us) on patrol, spotted the enemy about 2,000 feet over the bay. He gave the "tallyho" and his men dove to attack. When the Corsairs were within two miles of their targets, they were spotted and the Japanese scattered to the wind.

The Zeroes made section join ups and headed inland towards Cape Lambert to the east, full throttle. Hargrave's division of Corsairs turned in opposite directions and he lost visual contact. However, First Lieutenant Jean S. Patton Jr., leading the second division behind his skipper, saw all this and tried to radio him without success. Not about to loose his opportunity to score, Patton went in for the kill.

The VMF-216 mission report described the encounter:

"Lt. Patton's division picked out three of the Zekes and just as they were about to close, the enemy split up going three different directions. Patton closed with one that had pulled up in a gentle climb to the right, firing one long burst when just within range. The Zeke started to

Capt. Robert W. Wilson of VMF-222. (Credit: National Archives)

smoke and went into a spin to the right. Lt. Patton did not follow, but seeing a Zeke that Lieutenants Redmond and Mitch were chasing, turn inside them and come out just below, headed out to sea, Patton dove to the right and whipped in on its tail, closed to within range and fired several bursts from five and six o'clock and saw his tracers hit aft of the engine cowling, and then the left wing near the root. As the Zeke lost speed the engine, then left wing started burning and cockpit burst into flames. The enemy fighter then nosed over and dove straight down, crashing into sea eight or nine miles north of Cape Laguan. The remaining two Zekes managed to escape."[8]

Although the description of this Zero's demise is detailed, official Japanese records plus a couple of Zero pilots' accounts indicate that only two Zeroes were lost that day and both went down over Tobera.

1. Samuel Eliot Morrison, *History of United States Naval Operations in World War II*, Volume II, Little, Brown and Company, Boston, 1950, 423.
2. *U.S.S.B.S.*, 58-59.
3. Correspondence with Major General Robert P. Keller, 1984.
4. Ibid., 1992.
5. VMF-217 War Diary, March 1944.
6. Correspondence with Fumio Wako, 10 January 1992.
7. Correspondence with Robert W. Wilson, 1984.
8. Combat Tour of Duty of Marine Fighting Squadron Two Sixteen, March 1944, 11.

# 8

# RABAUL'S TOROKINA CAMPAIGN

A string of strategic defeats, starting with Midway, had pushed the Japanese further up the Solomon Island chain. The 4th Marine Raider Battalion landed on the southern tip of New Georgia Island on 21 June 1943.

On 30 June, the American 43rd Infantry Division captured Rendova Island, and all-important Munda Airfield fell on 5 August, compliments of the 43rd, 25th, and 37th Infantry Divisions. The Seabees (Naval construction battalion) went to work immediately improving the airfield even before its far end was secured. The Marines of VMF-123 and 124 began operating from Munda Airfield nine days later.[1] To the west, the intense Allied air offensive in New Guinea resulted in the capture of Lae and Salamaua in mid -September.

After Admiral Halsey had taken New Georgia, he decided to bypass Kolombangara - which was sandwiched in between New Georgia and Vella LaVella. As far as he was concerned, there was really no need to storm the island. He would simply starve the enemy into submission by isolating them. The Americans landed on Vella LaVella on 15 August and found virtually no resistance.[2]

With Halsey ramrodding his forces up the Slot, the Japanese had no choice but to fall back. They abandoned the Central Solomons and dug in on Bougainville. General Harukichi Hyakutake's 17th Army, some 40,000 strong, evacuated Guadalcanal by destroyers and decided to make their last stand on Bougainville.

On 1 November 1943, the Marines waded ashore at Empress Augusta Bay on Bougainville. The Japanese garrison fled into the jungles and the Americans set to work building an airstrip.

Allied Forces had island-hopped all the way up the Solomons and were now on Rabaul's doorstep. That doorstep was a group of small islands 117 miles east of Rabaul, known as Green Island (Nissan Island to the Japanese). It was stormed by the Third New Zealand Division on 15 February 1944 under an umbrella of Marine air cover. Within five days, the island was secured, and by 7 March, its airfield was ready to stage bombing attacks against Rabaul.

Rabaul HQ was so threatened by the fall of Green Island that they ordered a night bombing attack against the new airfield. Such an order was unreasonable under the circumstances, the aircrews having no night flying experience. While their bravery was not in question, the pilots knew their limitations and were reluctant to sortie.

It was a pathetic mission. At 0230 on 13 March, Warrant Officer Shigeo Fukumoto lifted his A6M off from Tobera's airstrip, followed by Petty Officers Yasushi Shimbo, Sekizen Shibayama, and Masajiro Kawato.[3] The unit had lost two precious Zeroes earlier in the afternoon in the scrap with Marines over Tobera. The apprehensive pilots tried desperately to locate each other in the vast darkness.

"We took off in bad weather with two 60 kg bombs," recalled Kawato. "We were supposed to assemble over Cape St. George. I thought there would be some light. I flew around and around, but didn't see one aircraft."[4]

Unable to join on their leader, three pilots aborted and landed. The veteran Fukumoto, determined to fulfill his assignment, forged ahead, completed his mission and returned.[5]

Rabaul had even bigger problems than Green Island. It became a matter of top priority that the Marine airfield at Torokina on Bougainville be re-captured by General Hyakutake's troops to relieve the pressure on Rabaul. Equally important was revenge for the humiliating defeat on Guadalcanal. Thus, the long and grueling march toward Torokina began around the end of December 1943. Lugging heavy artillery and equipment through the steaming jungles took a heavy toll.

On 8 March 1944, the Japanese began shelling the Torokina perimeter in one of the heaviest artillery barrages of the Pacific War. This stirred up a hornet's nest as the Americans retaliated by dropping sixty tons of bombs on the attackers. Hyakutake sent an urgent request to Rabaul for air support. His situation was tenuous. The best Rabaul HQ could do was to study the situation and stall for time.

Four American battleships were lurking around the Kavieng area on 20 March 1944. *New Mexico, Mississippi, Tennessee*, and *Idaho*, commanded by Rear Admiral Robert M. Griffin, were steaming toward Kavieng in a feint designed to fool the Japanese into thinking the invasion of New Ireland was imminent. Actually, the main thrust was to capture Emirau Island, which lay between Kavieng and the Admiralties. Tagging along were two escort carriers and fifteen destroyers.[6]

Ten Zeroes were quickly scrambled from Tobera to molest the American battleships, but the entire mission became an exercise in tactical self-abuse. Passing south of Vunakanau, the Zero formation was fired upon by their own anti-aircraft batteries. Warrant Of-

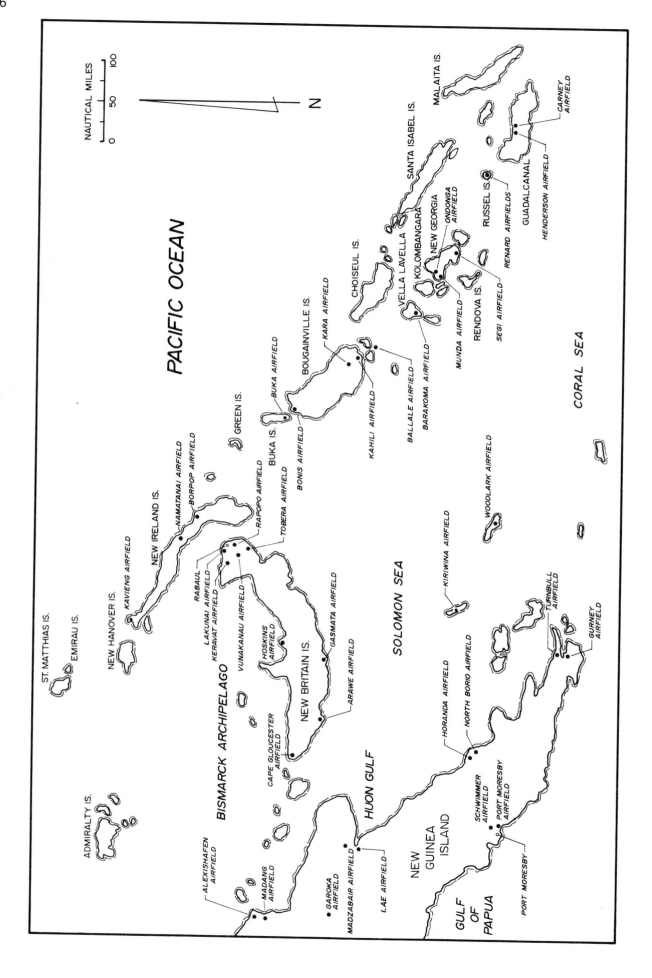

NAUTICAL MILES

0  50  100

N

PACIFIC OCEAN

ST. MATTHIAS IS.

EMIRAU IS.

ADMIRALTY IS.

NEW HANOVER IS.

KAVIENG AIRFIELD

NEW IRELAND IS.

NAMATANAI AIRFIELD

BORPOP AIRFIELD

BISMARCK ARCHIPELAGO

GREEN IS.

RAPOPO AIRFIELD

TOBERA AIRFIELD

RABAUL

LAKUNAI AIRFIELD

KERAVAT AIRFIELD

VUNAKANAU AIRFIELD

HOSKINS AIRFIELD

NEW BRITAIN IS.

GASMATA AIRFIELD

ARAWE AIRFIELD

CAPE GLOUCESTER AIRFIELD

BUKA AIRFIELD

BUKA IS.

BONIS AIRFIELD

BOUGAINVILLE IS.

KARA AIRFIELD

KAHILI AIRFIELD

BALLALE AIRFIELD

BARAKOMA AIRFIELD

CHOISEUL IS.

SANTA ISABEL IS.

MALAITA IS.

CARNEY AIRFIELD

GUADALCANAL

HENDERSON AIRFIELD

RENARD AIRFIELDS

RUSSEL IS.

NEW GEORGIA

ONDONGA AIRFIELD

KOLOMBANGARA

MUNDA AIRFIELD

VELLA LAVELLA

RENDOVA IS.

SEGI AIRFIELD

CORAL SEA

SOLOMON SEA

WOODLARK AIRFIELD

KIRIWINA AIRFIELD

TURNBULL AIRFIELD

GURNEY AIRFIELD

HORANDA AIRFIELD

NORTH BORIO AIRFIELD

SCHWIMMER AIRFIELD

PORT MORESBY AIRFIELD

PORT MORESBY

GULF OF PAPUA

NEW GUINEA ISLAND

HUON GULF

LAE AIRFIELD

MADZABAIR AIRFIELD

GAROKA AIRFIELD

MADANG AIRFIELD

ALEXISHAFEN AIRFIELD

ficer Fukumoto's Zero was hit and he made a successful emergency landing. The rest of the planes scattered through the flak like pigeons and unable to regroup, returned to base. In the meantime, the American battleships relandscaped Kavieng with 1,079 rounds of 14-inch and 12,281 rounds of five-inch shells.

When the Zeroes returned to base, they were quickly checked over and sent on their way again but once more failed to locate their objective and returned home.[8]

General Hyakutake's hand was now quickly being pulled into the American meat grinder and he was screaming for air support; Rabaul was forced to act. Their first night attack on 13 March against Green Island had not been very inspiring. Captain Soji Ikari, commander of Tobera Airfield, ordered Warrant Officer Fukumoto to pick out pilots for another try. Petty Officer Sekizen Shibayama volunteered to lead the flight. In the early morning hours of 21 March, six Zeroes led by Shibayama attempted the impossible.

"In those days, we weren't equipped to fly at night," recalls Shibayama. "We did not have radios and we lacked night training. As soon as we took off, two of them returned because of some troubles." Shibayama made it as far as Cape St. George; the others failed to link up.[9]

Shibayama knew that the mission had failed. It was still pitch black and he could not land, so he jettisoned his bombs into the sea and bided his time until dawn, then landed and reported to the commander. Petty Officer Yoshio Otsuki also flew around Rabaul for several hours until he could land. The others had already touched down.[10] It was painfully obvious by this time that the fighter pilots were terribly deficient in night navigation and formation flying.

The 17th Army planned a last Banzai attack against the Americans at Torokina on the night of 23-24 March 1944 and demanded air support. Captain Ikari promised some cover and Warrant Officer Fukumoto briefed the pilots on their assignments.

The mission got off to a bad start. During takeoff at 0230, one Zero skidded to the side, colliding with two others. Scratch three Zeroes. Petty Officer Sekizen Shibayama was once again in the lead, but bad weather forced the leader and another to return. The lone aircraft, piloted by Petty Officer First Class Masaru Tsukiji, flew on toward Torokina and was never heard from again.

General Hyakutake's last big push to capture the Torokina airfields ended in dismal failure; the remnants fled back into the jungle in wild disorder, leaving behind 5,469 dead. Captain Ikari failed to deliver on his promise and lost face. Warrant Officer Fukumoto, who had briefed the pilots but did not fly the mission, was called before the irate commander and slapped.[11]

With the pressure at Torokina gone, the Americans stepped up the bombardment of Rabaul.

PO Sekizen Shibayama in the cockpit of a Type 96 fighter. He was a flight instructor before assignment to Rabaul. (Credit: Shibayama)

1. *History of Marine Corps Aviation in World War II*, Combat Forces Press, Washington, 1952, 155.
2. Ibid., 156
3. Jin-Ichi Kusaka, *Rabaul Sen Sen Ijo Nashi* (All Quiet on the Rabaul Front), Kowa-Do Publishers, Tokyo, Japan, 1958. Vice Admiral Kusaka gives the takeoff time as 0230 which is confirmed by Kawato in his memoir Zero-Sen Rabaul Ni Ari. Kawato lists the flight leader as "Shibata." Actually, "Shibata" was Sekizen Shibayama, who confirmed leading this mission in a letter to the author in 1993.
4. *Zero-Sen Rabaul Ni Ari.*
5. Ibid.
6. Action Report - Bombardment of Kavieng, 20 March 1944, Commander Task Force 37, A16-3, Serial 043.
7. *History of United States Naval Operations in World War II*, Volume II, 423.
8. Flight records of Rabaul's aircraft for 20 March 1944 shows 17 sorties flown, but no losses nor details are given. According to an unsubstantiated story appearing in Maru Magazine (Saigo No Rabaul Zero Sen Tai Kito Seiri - Last Zero Squadron Return Safely), 1975, seven Zeroes attacked a small carrier near Kavieng on the afternoon mission and claimed a near hit. However, according to official American records, this incident never occurred. The Action Report - Bombardment of Kavieng states that a "Tony" fighter was shot down when it approached within 45 miles of the *Natoma Bay*.
9. Correspondence from Sekizen Shibayama, 17 January 1992.
10. Ibid.
11. Ibid.

# 9

# NIGHT FIGHTERS

The heavy dosage bombardments of Rabaul during October and November 1943 had failed to bring it to its knees. By the Spring of 1944, bombing the Japanese bastion had become a sadistic ritual. "Daisy Cutters" (high explosive bombs used to flatten acres of ground), parafrags (parachute fragmentation bombs), and time-delayed bombs rained down on the hapless defenders. The Marines used depth charges with Daisy Cutter fuses so they would explode above ground.[1] Ingenious Americans reveled in innovative ways of inflicting death on their foes.

"American time-delayed parachute bombs were small sized and they didn't menace us so much, " remembers Commander Tomoyoshi Hori. "But we were annoyed by the disposal of them. We detonated the bombs from a safe distance with machine gun fire, but there were many bombs out of sight, which were hidden in the bushes or out in the field. I heard quite a few men were killed and wounded by such bombs."[2]

During the month of March 1944, the seaplane 958th Air Group, which had been exempted from the Truk withdrawal, was picking up the slack for the badly mauled Zero squadron. Lieutenant Kozo Numakawa, who served as a squadron leader, described their situation:

"At the end of February 1944, after the Petes had gone to Truk, eight Jakes remained at Rabaul. The Matupi Island base had been abandoned on account of Allied bombing and strafing, and two planes were kept just west of Praed Point. These aircraft were drawn up among the coconut palms on the shore and camouflaged with nets and grass. At the time they were held in reserve, and the other six aircraft, which were being used, were kept at Malaguna."[3]

The 958th had started off 1944 badly. One of their floatplanes was lost on 3 January during a convoy mission. The next morning at 0945, Lieutenant (j.g.) Donald E. Runyon of VF-18 shot down a twin-float Jake ten miles northeast of Kavieng. In mid-February, three more Jakes vanished within a week. They were falling victim to a calculating predator, a vicious nightstalker unit.

VMF(N)-531 was the first Marine night fighter squadron in the South Pacific. It received its commission in November 1942 at Cherry Point, North Carolina. From Guadalcanal, they moved up to Vella Lavella, Bougainville, and Green Island. Their presence in the Rabaul area was a minor miracle in itself; they had been plagued all through training with shortages of aircraft, spare parts, and learning the intricacies of radar and night fighting. Now, they were gaining experience through trial and error and on the job training, utilizing the 958th's seaplane scouts as targets.

The new pioneers in Marine aviation fought hard to justify their formation. Night fighting was an unknown science and not everyone supported it. VMF(N)-531 had initially hoped to get their hands on the Army's new P-61 Black Widow. It seemed perfect for the Marine Corps

**The widely used float reconnaissance Aichi E13A Jake was employed by Rabaul's 958th Air Group. (Depiction by Shori Tanaka)**

A Lockheed PV-1 Ventura on Bougainville in 1944. (Credit: National Archives)

image: powerful, deadly, and macho. As a new Marine outfit, they were engaged in wishful thinking as the Marines rarely got what they really wanted. What they received instead was the PV-1 Ventura, an aesthetically incorrect twin-engine Lockheed Hudson look alike. If the P-61 was a hotrod, the Ventura was an Edsel – functional and uncool.

VMF(N)-531 scored its first night victory on 13 November 1943 when Captain Duane R. Jenkins and his crew downed a Betty bomber fifty miles southwest of Torokina.[4] They started biting into the 958th on 15 February 1944. Colonel Frank Schwable and his crew (Sergeants William J. Fletcher and Robert I. Ward) shot down a Jake ten miles northeast of Kavieng. Two nights later, on 17 February at 0505, Schwable and his crew chalked up another off Green Island. Another Ventura, piloted by First Lieutenant Jack M. Plunkett, and crewed by Staff Sergeants Floyd M. Pulham and Michael J. Cipkala claimed a Jake at 0330 ten miles west of Green Island. Although VMF(N)-531 claimed two victories that night, only one Jake was lost. Two nights later, Lieutenant Colonel John Harshberger and his crew retired another 958th aircraft twenty-five miles southwest of Green Island.

The Marine night stalkers were not the only problems confronting the 958th. The US Navy's Motor Torpedo Boat Squadrons 7, 12, and 25, based at Dreger Harbor, New Guinea (south of Finschafen) were making their presence known along the south coast of New Britain. This forced the 958th to increase patrols in the area. Occasional forays during the months of March and April netted the American PT boats nine supply barges, a lugger, and a small cargo ship. Jakes were ordered to search and destroy these pesky, thin-hulled wooden menaces.

On the night of 13-14 April 1944 Lieutenant (j.g.) Julius O. Aschenbach in PT 132, and Ensign Fendall M. Clagett in PT 133, ran into eight enemy barges in Henry Reid Bay (Wide Bay). As the two American vessels were busy sinking four, destroying two others on the beach, and damaging the remaining two, a Jake appeared overhead. It dropped its load of bombs, but missed then came back and made two strafing runs before vanishing into the darkness.[5]

The Japanese had claimed a number of enemy PT boats sunk by Jakes in fire fights around Rabaul and elsewhere. In reality, no PT boats were ever lost to a Jake. There may have been near misses, but darkness played strange tricks on all involved.

The Japanese had entered the night fighting arena at Rabaul in May 1943. The irritating night bombing raids by Allied bombers, especially B-17s, had to be challenged. While they caused very little physical damage, their unmolested forays over the great Japanese stronghold were embarrassing to the Navy. Commander Yasuna Kozono, commanding officer of the 251st Air Group, came up with an idea to combat the nocturnal nuisance.

PT 132 of the US Navy on patrol in 1945. With a plywood hull these vessels could exceed 45 knots. (Credit: PT Boat, Inc.)

A J1N1-S Irving, ("Gekko" to the Japanese) night fighter taxis at an unknown location. (Credit: National Archives via Jim Lansdale)

In May, two twin-engined Nakajima J1N1 Gekko fighters (Allied codename: Irving) were prepared as night fighters. Kozono ordered the installation of two fixed 20mm cannons behind the observer's position, pointed upward at 30 degrees. The radical idea was for the aircraft to position itself underneath the enemy bomber and fire into its less protected belly! The Gekko did not utilize radar to find their prey relying instead on ground searchlights or moonlight to silhouette their targets. The pilot and observer were given injections to aid their night vision.[6]

Commander Kozono's wild scheme paid off immediately. In the early morning hours of 21 May 1943,

Rabaul's "King of the Night", PO 1/c Shigetoshi Kudo, just after being awarded a ceremonial sword from Adm. Kusaka in July 1943. (Credit: K. Osuo)

Chief Petty Officer Shigetoshi Kudo and Lieutenant (j.g.) Akira Sugawara (observer) caught a B-17 illuminated by searchlights. Sliding underneath the Flying Fortress, Kudo pumped his cannon fire into the unsuspecting bomber. Major Paul Williams and his crew from the 64th Bomb Squadron fell to their deaths shortly after 0337 in the St. George's Channel.

At 0428, the other Irving team (CPO Satoru Ono and observer, Lieutenant (j.g.) Kisaku Hamano) blasted B-17 #41-9011 out of the sky.[7]

When bombers failed to return, the Americans assumed that they had been lost to anti-aircraft fire or operational mishaps. Kudo claimed eight bombers in a two month period including two Flying Fortresses on the night of 26 June 1943. One of his victims lived to tell the tale.

First Lieutenant Jose L. "Joe" Holguin, navigator aboard #41-2430, didn't know what hit them. The mission of this 65th Bomb Squadron, 43rd Bomb Group B-17, was to bomb Vunakanau Airfield. Since they had no idea that the Japanese had night fighters, the sortie was not considered very hazardous. Anti-aircraft fire was predictably inaccurate.

As bombs were streaking earthward from "Naughty But Nice," searchlights illuminated it, but the crew felt little danger. Suddenly, 20mm cannon shells punctured the Flying Fortress, exploding within and sending shrapnel and debris through the cramped interior. The copilot was killed instantly and slumped forward. Holguin looked around and saw death everywhere. The night fighter team of Kudo and Michitaro Ichikawa (observer) raked the underside of the B-17 with deadly precision. Metal fragments hit Holguin, a young man from the barrios of East Los Angeles, in the chin; another piece tore through his left leg. With two engines on fire the aircraft nosed down.

The great Flying Fortress began a deadly spin. Holguin was attempting to help a crewman strap on his parachute when he was sucked out of an open escape hatch. Tumbling through the pitch blackness and disoriented, Holguin made two pulls on the ripcord and was given life. He landed roughly through a tree, battered and bruised. In the morning, he inched his way to the wreckage of his beloved bomber and crew and found

Seven of these men died on the night of 26 Jun 1943 when their B-17, "Naughty But Nice" was downed by Rabaul's night fighter ace, CPO Shigetoshi Kudo. They are (L. to R.) Top row: Jose L. Holguin (sole survivor), Hal Winfrey (pilot not on mission), Charles Trimingham, Frank Peattie. Bottom row: Robert Griebel, Leonard Gionet, Robert Christopherson, Pace Payng and Henry Garcia. (Credit: Curt Holguin)

that all were dead. With a broken back, Holguin survived for more than twenty-seven days in the wild until friendly natives carried him to their village. He was later turned over to the 6th Field Kempei Tai (Army military police) to serve the rest of the war in their POW camp.[8]

Shigetoshi Kudo, who shot down Holguin and his crew, earned the title of "King of the Night." He was presented with a ceremonial sword from Admiral Kusaka for distinguished service. He later saw combat in the home defense and ended the war with nine victories. He died in 1960 as a result of injuries suffered in a 1945 landing accident. Kudo's observer, Michitaro Ichikawa, died in July 1994 at the age of seventy-six.

In July 1943, the Gekkos were transferred to Ballale where they were badly needed and the team of Kudo-Sugawara continued to increase their scores. A few of the night fighters were sent to Kavieng and some operated out of Rabaul. By February 1944, only four inoperable aircraft remained at Rabaul.

Engineers worked tirelessly on the derelicts and by the end of the month, one came on line. Shortly afterwards, another became operational. These two night fighters made a total of eleven sorties in the month of March, but apparently made no claims nor contacts. So important were these orphaned planes that their use was controlled directly by Rabaul Headquarters.

The first combat between the refurbished Gekkos and the Americans occurred on the night of 8 April 1944. The Marines had a North American PBJ snooper over Rabaul when they came under attack by

a twin-engined fighter, initially identified as a Japanese Army Ki-45 (Nick). Captain Robert Millington of VMB-413, pilot of the lone Mitchell, did not realize what was waiting for him.

"I was over the target forty minutes, from 2200 to 2240, when I came under attack," re-

Capt. Robert Millington of VMB-413 at Espirtu Santo, June 1944. (Credit: R. Millington)

**PBJ-1Ds of VMB-413 en route from Sterling Island to Rabaul. Note ASG under-belly radar bowl. The Marine Mitchell squadrons flew both day and night missions. (Credit: Bob Millington)**

calls Millington. "It was a moonlight night and we had been through the 'lights' twice and were on a bombing run at 10,000 feet when my tailgunner said, 'Captain, aren't we supposed to be up here alone?', to which I responded, 'That's right, Mert.' And he said, 'Well, we ain't. There's a plane coming up under us!' I'm afraid I was too damned dumb to realize the danger we were all in at that point and so I continued on my bombing run, telling my gunner, 'When he gets close enough, let him have it.' Shortly, my gunner said, 'Captain, he's shooting at us!', to which I replied, 'Well, shoot back.' Then he came back on and said, 'Captain, I can't depress my gun far enough!'"[9]

The Japanese night fighter was positioning itself right underneath the Mitchell for the kill. Millington and his crew had seconds to live.

"At that point, I did a ninety degree turn and got clear of him," adds Millington. "My turret gunner, L.E. Tommy Thomas had a perfect shot at 100 yards, and his turret wouldn't work. Unfortunately, the turret had somehow been damaged by flak on a morning sortie. Tommy was pretty sick about it because it was the only shot he had the whole war and he said he couldn't have missed."[10]

PBJ #43-B22 with one very jaded turret gunner returned safely to base. "But for the Grace of God, he would have shot my plane down, and but for the Grace of God, my gunners might have gotten him," recalled Millington.[11]

The same Gekko continued to make the rounds over Rabaul looking for action. PBJ #44-B22, piloted by Captain Frank Habig, sighted a bogey over Matupi Crater at 12,000 feet. The nightfighter came in from ten o'clock and hosed the Americans with its guns, then vanished.[12]

The Gekkos flew two more sorties, achieved no success, then flew on to Truk on 26 April 1944 to rejoin the 251st Air Group. Only one broken down aircraft remained at Rabaul and it would never be flown again on combat missions. On 8 November 1944, while on its way to Truk, it vanished.

Soon after the Japanese night fighters disappeared from the night sky over Rabaul, the personal battle between VMF(N)-531 and the Jakes may have finally played itself out at 0437 on 11 May 1944. A PV-1 piloted by First Lieutenant Marvin E. Notestine, and carrying Sergeant Edward H. Benintende (radar operator), and Corporal W.M. Kinn, located a float plane as it was coming back to Rabaul from patrol.

Edward Benintende noted the following in his diary:

"On snoop patrol in vicinity of Rabaul. At 0320 we sighted PT boats AA fire at a bogey. We investigated and found nothing. 0437 we sighted a bogey in a head-on approach, 200 feet below us, one and one-half miles ahead. We were at 400 feet and the bogey made a ninety degree port turn which brought him directly approaching Simpson Harbor. We made a 270 degree port turn which brought us directly astern of the bogey following his course. Bogey made his landing approach, navigation lights on when he was abreast (port) of Matupi Island. We dove on him and strafed him from above. A well aimed burst of approximately thirty-five rounds per gun was a direct hit. There were numerous incendiary bullet flashes on bogey and he blew up in a great flash of light immediately as we passed over him."[13]

The 958th did not record a loss that night nor anytime during the month of May. It may have been a visitor from Buin. Something went down and this was recorded as VMF(N)-531's twelfth and final victory.

"I'm not sure what I can add that would be of any interest except for my own personal feelings of anticipation in the possible destruction of an enemy aircraft which was our purpose in being in the Pacific," says Benintende. "Then there was the fear of being shot down in the crossfire so prevalent over Rabaul Harbor. I felt that we were luckier than the occupants of the Jake. And because we stayed in the area long after our patrol was scheduled to end, there was a rather tumultuous welcome for us after we buzzed the tower. Other members of the squadron thought that we were lost because we were so late in returning."

"I truly hope that there are no Japanese who are interested in knowing who manned the PV-1 who destroyed the Jake. We were all where we were because of pure chance...I must say that I had no thoughts about our adversaries as people with feelings and aspirations of their own. We were there to do a job and we left it at that...I took great comfort in the anonymity of the air war. Members of infantry units frequently had to look at their adversaries face to face and I am thankful for being spared that kind of confrontational situation."[14]

The Japanese anticipated enemy landings on Gazelle Peninsula, so three Jakes were used every night to monitor the situation. Later, the number of floatplanes were reduced to one. Finally in June, this mission was abandoned, but not before loosing another Jake in a fire fight with a PT boat in the Kavieng area.

1. Correspondence with Bob Millington, 1993.
2. Correspondence with Tomoyoshi Hori, 1 March 1993.
3. Interrogation of Japanese Air Crew, Appendix D3, 7.
4. VMF(N)-531 War Diary and Aircraft Action Report for 13 November 1943.
5. Motor Torpedo Boat Squadron Seven War Diary for 13 April 1944.
6. B-17 navigator Jose L. Holguin's conversations with Rabaul nightfighter pilot Satoru Ono, April 1988, Tokyo, Japan. The author was not able to discover what substance was used for injections.
7. Robert C. Mikesh and Osamu Tagaya, *Moonlight Interceptor, Japan's "Irving" Night Fighter*, Smithsonian Institution Press, Washington DC, 1985, xiii, xv, 37.
8. Unpublished memoir of Jose L. Holguin, 1988.
9. Millington correspondence.
10. Ibid.
11. Ibid.
12. Flight log of Rabaul Headquarters for 8 November 1944.
13. War diary of Edward Benintende for 11 May 1944.
14. Correspondence with Edward Benintende, 24 January 1993.

**Saturation bombing of Rabaul on 22 March 1944 gutted the wharf and downtown areas. (Credit: National Archives)**

# 10

# THE WAR OF NERVES

The Marine Corps, traditional stepchild of the US Navy when it came to allocation of scarce equipment, had long sought multi-engine shore-based aircraft – a break with the flying boat era. The US aircraft production "horn of plenty" finally disgorged the long awaited planes rather by chance than by any strategic policy decision. The Marines received some 700 North American B-25 Mitchells, mostly D,H and J models beginning in 1943. They were redesignated PBJ, and the Marines were delighted with their new offensive weapon.

Six PBJ bombing units were quickly raised. VMB-413 was the first to see action and pioneered the way for others to follow. On 3 March 1944 they arrived on Stirling Island and commenced offensive operations on the 15th.

Robert Millington, now an attorney in Gridley, California, was a member of VMB-413. He remembers:

"We flew PBJ-1D's (B-25-D's)...We were radar equipped with an A.S. George radar with a 360 degree scope in the belly of the plane where the bottom turret had been. We flew daylight mission every third day, but our general duty was to keep one plane over Rabaul and/or Kavieng from sundown until sunup. We would fly anywhere from six to nine planes a night for this purpose and would be armed with fourteen 100 pound bombs plus as many twenty pound anti-personnel bombs as the crew could store in the rear of the plane plus magnesium flares, plus all the empty beer bottles and Coke bottles we could get in the plane. Each plane would spend an hour to one and one half hours over the target making repeated runs dropping the various ordnance – bombs, flares, and coke bottles in order to keep the Japs awake."[1]

VMB-413's second night mission to Rabaul, on 22 March 1944, was to "heckle Rabaul singularly at hourly intervals"[2] and they had ten PBJs lined up for the exercise. Aircraft No. 24 was the first off at 1823, piloted by Major James K. Smith and carrying Captain John F. Jackson, Second Lieutenant Frank Just Jr., and Corporals Francis X. Nuwer, Willard M. Lytle, and Harold T. Nelson. They were to arrive over their destination at 2000 hours (1900 hours Rabaul time) from St. George's Channel.

Major Smith had been a poor choice to fly this mission. He had come to the squadron as a captain and flight officer, lacking twin-engined training. He had flown floatplanes off Guantanamo, but the PBJ was much more demanding. During a check flight with Lieutenant Ed Cornwell, Smith had gone into a "graveyard spiral" which convinced Cornwell that the major was not qualified to fly instruments.[3]

Four Zero pilots were conducting training exercises at dusk when they spotted the approach of a lone twin-engined bomber coming in over the channel; there was just enough light left to identify the intruder as a B-25. It was Major Smith's PBJ cruising leisurely

A PBJ Mitchell of VMB-423 on a mission to Rabaul. (Credit: Wm. Hopper)

**Maj. James "Ken" Smith (top) and fellow crew members, Capt. John F. Jackson (left) and 2nd Lt. Frank Just, Jr. (right) of VMB-413, became victims of Rabaul's guerrila air force. (Credit: Bob Millington)**

at 4,500 feet, oblivious to the four enemy fighters positioned 1,500 feet above. The crew was unaware that Rabaul still had combat-capable interceptors and had let their guard down.

With Petty Officer Fumio Wako in the lead, followed by Petty Officers Kentaro Miyagoshi, Takeshi Kaneko, and Masajiro Kawato, they pounced on the unsuspecting intruder. After a very brief return of fire, the PBJ slowed and began a gradual descent into the bay. Five men parachuted. Wako delivered the coup de grace and sent it crashing in flames.[4] So sudden was their demise that they failed to get off an SOS call. Another PBJ, piloted by Lieutenant William D. Graul also failed to return, lost in a fierce storm in the vicinity of Kieta, Bougainville.

"I was Officer of the Day the night Smith and Graul were lost," recalls Bob Millington. "I remember it well because I did not get to bed for 36 hours thereafter. I was 1st Lieutenant at the time, promoted to Captain ten days later. There was a storm that night of March 22, 1944, that was as bad as any I have ever seen in the South Pacific area...Smith's plane was the first one off, at about 6:00pm, to the best of my memory. He was the operations or flight officer of the squadron at the time. I was not on duty down at the strip at the time he took off in the storm. Of course, being a Major, he made his own decisions."[5]

On learning in 1992 that Major Smith's PBJ was downed by four Zeroes, Millington was shocked. He had always assumed that they had been lost in bad weather. "We have always wondered about Major J.K. Smith and his crew," said Millington.[6]

The intensity of continued Allied bombing of Tobera Airfield made operations almost impossible. TBF Avengers attacked runways while the SBD dive bombers hit gun emplacements. Low flying B-25s delivered time-delayed parachute bombs. Their parting gifts caused havoc with ground crews assigned to repair the airfield. B-24 Liberators with their huge bomb capacity just added to the misery. The Zero pilots abandoned Tobera and went to Vunakanau Airfield, which was a superior operating base.

Yoshinobu Ikeda, a pilot in the squadron, recalls those terrible days:

"The Americans bombed the hell out of us and changed the landscape; the trees and palms were all blasted out. Now that I think about it, it was a losing battle."[7]

Warrant Officer Shigeo Fukumoto, the squadron's most experienced pilot, was ordered to take the last four remaining Zeroes and escort two twin-engined night fighters to Truk. They bade farewell to Rabaul on 25 April 1944. The next day, a third night fighter departed. While Fukumoto's leadership would be missed, the others remaining behind had proven themselves in combat and could now fend for themselves.

Trained for the combat role, the Zero pilots were becoming restless. Their boredom was broken slightly on 1 May 1944, when four Zeroes on a training exercise chased a lone New Zealand PV-1 Ventura over St. George's Channel. Flight Sergeant H.V. Baker eluded the pack by disappearing into clouds.

Only one reconnaissance mission to the Admiralties was flown for the entire month of May by two Zeroes (Shimbo and Kawato). The next mission, also to the Admiralties by two Zeroes, occurred on 6 June.[8] Orders had been given to avoid combat whenever possible; these custom-built Zeroes would be hard to replace. But the pilots were itching to prove themselves. The killer instinct, beaten into them throughout training, was hard to suppress.

The Marine bombing squadron on Green Island was unaware that Rabaul still had Zeroes. PBJ equipped VMB-423 had relieved VMB-413 on 15 May. On 9 June 1944, they got a rude shock.

Twenty-three year old Lieutenant William H. Hopper and crew departed Green Island at 1730. Sig Higgins, Hopper's copilot, recalls :

"Our squadron mission, at that time, was to be over the Rabaul area from 6 p.m. to 6 a.m., surveying the area with radar during the night, to either be aware of any ship or plane movement, and to harass by dropping bombs on any lights we might see."[9]

At 1810, the PBJ disgorged a hundred pounder on Tobera Airfield from 9,000 feet, but the effort went

On 9 June 1944 this VMB-423 Mitchell bomber crew encountered Zeros. L. to R.: Front, Sgts. Angelo Bilotta and William Wright. Standing, Sgt. Jimmie Young, Lt. Sig Higgins, Lt. William Hopper and Sgt. Ralph Fiorelli. (Credit: Wm. Hopper)

unrecognized. There was absolutely no response from anti-aircraft. The Japanese had gone totally underground by February and March 1944, their soldiers sleeping undisturbed in shelters. They had learned to live with the nocturnal nuisance and a few bombs were nothing to get excited about. Anti-aircraft batteries usually kept their silence for fear of letting the enemy know that their tactics were succeeding.

Hopper dropped another bomb on Lakunai Airfield to see what they could stir up. The crew encountered meager and inaccurate anti-aircraft fire, but nothing more. The snoop and heckle mission had become boring as the PBJ cruised leisurely to Vunakanau Airfield. At 1840 while circling the airfield at 10,000, they spotted two fighters below at 4,000 feet altitude. Chief Petty Officer Yasushi Shimbo and his wingman, Fumio Wako, were seen flying loops and doing rolls. The two pilots had been training when the opportunity (or excuse) for combat presented itself.

Lieutenant Hopper alerted his crew to be on the watch and ready for any action.

"The PBJ had a cruising speed of about 165-185 knots," writes Hopper. "We knew the fighters approached 300 knots, and could fly circles around us. My left thumb button controlled four forward firing .50 caliber machine guns. The navigator/bombardier had one .50, and the top turret had two. Thus, we could fire seven .50's forward."[10]

Shimbo looked up and couldn't believe his good fortune. A lone B-25! The pair of fighters roared up to 10,000 feet to do battle.

Angelo F. Bilotta, now of Pittsfield, Massachusetts remembers this action.

"Hopper decided to stay and fight because he didn't think we would have a chance if he tried to escape. So he went in and out of the cumulus clouds hoping that they wouldn't be waiting for us when we came out. While out of the clouds, he kept turning toward the planes and using all of the guns that we could bear forward (I was in the turret). How long doing this, fifteen to thirty minutes, I don't know, it seemed much longer."[11]

The two Zeroes made four runs on the PBJ. All runs were made in section right echelon with the wingman approximately twenty yards behind the leader.

"We kept turning toward the planes, or trying to, in order to bring all seven guns into play. We were never able to achieve our objective," comments Hopper.[12]

The two Zeroes climbed to approximately 3,000 feet above the American intruder and executed an overhead reverse run. As soon as they dove, they commenced firing. Hopper pulled up into a stall, then kicked his nose over and increased speed. This maneuver ruined his opponents' deflection shooting and the Zeros whipped past and disappeared into the clouds below. Their last pass made a memorable impression.

"The run I remember most (the last one) was a vertical dive from above and to the rear," recollects Bilotta. "The tracers looked as if they were going into the tail and until we heard from William Wright (tail gunner), we thought we had lost him. He later said the tracers were so close that he could reach out and grab them."[13]

At 1855, with darkness descending, the Zeroes called it quits and headed home. Marksmanship on both sides was abysmal - nobody hit anything. As soon as the Zeroes left, moderate anti-aircraft fire appeared, but did no damage.

Lt. William Hopper of VMB-423. (Credit: Hopper)

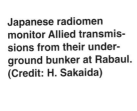
Japanese radiomen monitor Allied transmissions from their underground bunker at Rabaul. (Credit: H. Sakaida)

Hopper and crew went back to harassing enemy airfields. They dropped three more hundred pounders on Vunakanau during the night but the anti-aircraft guns remained strangely silent. They dropped their last bomb on Lakunai and returned safely to Green Island at 2125.[14]

Bill Hopper holds the distinction of being one of three Marine pilots in World War II to fly over 100 missions. He left the Marines with the rank of captain. Dr. William H. Hopper is now a retired justice educator and resides in Oakland, California.

1. Correspondence from Bob Millington, 1993.
2. VMB-413 Aircraft Action Report for 22-23 March 1944.
3. Correspondence from Ed Cornwell, 1993.
4. *Zero-Sen Rabaul Ni Ari*. According to Kawato's account, the date of this encounter was given around 7 March 1944. There were no losses of a lone Allied twin-engined bomber over Rabaul until the night of 22-23 which tallies with the loss of VMB-413's PBJ. Fumio Wako confirmed the destruction of this PBJ in a letter dated 6 January 1992. A copy of Kawato's memoir was sent to his comrade, Yoshinobu Ikeda. In his response dated 19 May 1994, Ikeda expressed "shock" that there were four Zeroes involved. He had always believed that Wako was flying alone when this action occurred. Kawato wrote in his memoir that five crewmem parachuted out. They were undoubtedly captured by the Japanese Navy, interrogated, then executed. Millington questioned whether there was enough light for the Japanese pilots to engage. Peter Woodbury of Sydney, Australia checked into this. There was a full moon on 10 March 1944 and a new moon on 24 March. Although there was no moonlight on the 22nd, there must have been just a little light left around seven o'clock Rabaul time.
5. Millington.
6. Ibid.
7. Correspondence with Yoshinobu Ikeda, 1992.
8. Flight record of Rabaul's aircraft for May and June 1944.
9. Correspondence from Sig Higgins, 1993.
10. Correspondence from William H. Hopper, 1992.
11. Correspondence from Angelo F. Bilotta, 25 May 1992.
12. Hopper.
13. Bilotta
14. VMB-423 Aircraft Action Report, Report No.32, 9 June 1944

VMB-423 Insignia

# 11

# THE LAST MARINE VICTORY

Rabaul HQ felt a need to reconnoiter the Admiralties to determine what Allied Forces were planning. The 5th Air Base Squadron on Truk loaned a pair of Zeroes to assist and these aircraft flew a mission to the Admiralties on 31 May 1944.[1] They brought back information that Allied Forces had established airfields (Momote and Mokerang) on Los Negros. This was bad news for Rabaul.

Marine Corps fighter pilots flying missions to Rabaul were becoming bored with the lack of enemy opposition. Their last victory had been on 12 March. Bomber escort missions and strafing were no substitute for Zeroes. They felt cheated as the war was passing them by.

As the Marines sat by the sidelines, their Army counterparts were scoring heavily to the west in New Guinea. P-38s and P-47s decimated entire enemy air units. By 25 July 1944, the USAAF had buried the Japanese Army's 68th, 77th, 78th, and the 248th Air Groups. Major Richard Bong had racked up 28 victories to take the lead in the scoring race.

Politics began playing a big role in who got the glory. First Lieutenant John M. Foster of VMF-222 recalled:

"We received orders from General MacArthur prohibiting us from attacking the enemy on New Britain south of a line drawn on the maps, which deprived us of the happy hunting ground at Wide Bay. That area was to be considered part of the Southwest Pacific Area and we were to confine ourselves to the South Pacific Area."[2]

"Actually, we were all under MacArthur from about Munda on," said former Marine PBJ pilot Bob Millington. "I well remember reading daily bulletins concerning Army Air Force activities over Rabaul. The Marine, Navy, and New Zealanders were not mentioned. They said MacArthur's Air Force did this and such. This didn't go down too well."[3]

By this time the Japanese rear guard 253rd had two operable Zeroes and two veterans well enough to sortie. Petty Officers Yasushi Shimbo and Masajiro Kawato volunteered for the hazardous assignment. On 6 June, they flew to the Admiralty Islands and reported over 300 aircraft parked on runways, three aircraft carriers, four battleships, plus numerous supply and transport ships docked in the harbor. They returned to Vunakanau in the late afternoon without mishap.[4]

13 June 1944 was to be a memorable day for the Marines. On this day, Rabaul again dispatched two Zeroes for a reconnaissance of the Admiralties. Unfortunately, they were forced by bad weather to abort and one tried to land on Kavieng. Then along came Second Lieutenant Roland B. Heilman of VMF-222 and his wingman.

**Vought F4U-1 Corsairs of VMF-223 on Green Island in March 1944. (Credit: Tailhook)**

Vice Adm. Kusaka (front row, center) and his staff, April 1944. (Credit: Naotaro Kusaka)

"I remember that weather prevented air operations over Emirau Island that day," explains Heilman of that long ago encounter. "We had heavy rain and thunderstorms until afternoon. Pat Dugan and I were assigned to patrol Kavieng from VMF-222, and Major Ted Wojcik and a Lieutenant Lathrop from VMF-211 were assigned to patrol about thirty miles to the northwest. Kavieng had an airstrip surrounded by a concentration of anti-aircraft positions (around ninety), an auxiliary airstrip, or perhaps an incomplete strip lay to the southeast (Namatanai, I believe) near Fangelawea Bay.

"We were aware of some air activity in the New Britain, New Ireland area but hadn't been able to catch them. For this reason, I planned the flight to patrol at high altitude and arrived over Kavieng at between 14,000 and 15,000 feet. Just as we came abreast of the airstrip I spotted a Zero just becoming airborne. Because of the possibility the Zero was a lure, we circled and scanned the sky. The enemy pilot seemed to put on a show for the ground crew. He buzzed down one side of the strip, made a tight turn and buzzed the other side. Meanwhile, we jettisoned our bombs, charged guns and let down to about 8,000 or 9,000 feet. As we watched, the Zero turned south and began a wide circle to the left which took him near the Namatanai strip and out over the bay.

"I was in position to attack as he crossed the shoreline so we dropped on him in a steep dive. I fired a long burst which seemed to cover the area of the engine back to the cockpit. The aircraft nosed over and plunged into the water a mile or more offshore. The pilot did not bail out and I do not believe he could have survived the crash. His altitude when we attacked was 1,500 to 2,000 feet, and he went down flaming from the right side."[5]

The Zero, one of those on loan from Truk, became VMF-222's last aerial victory in the South Pacific Campaign. It was Roland Heilman's first and only victory in World War II.

1. **Correspondence from Tomoyoshi Hori, 19 September 1993.**
2. *Hell in the Heavens*, **344-345.**
3. **Correspondence from Bob Millington, 1993.**
4. *Zero-Sen Rabaul Ni Ari.*
5. **Correspondence from Roland B. Heilman, 27 October1992**

# 12

# 105th NAVAL BASE AIR UNIT

On 15 June 1944, the ragtag Zero squadron at Rabaul was attached to the newly formed 105th Naval Base Air Unit. The transfer of the 253rd's rear guard force to the 105th was purely an administrative move. The once powerful 253rd was disbanded on 10 July 1944 after suffering a series of crippling defeats.[1]

Vice Admiral Jin-Ichi Kusaka's Eleventh Air Fleet, once the terror of the South Pacific, was now represented by a handful of motley aircraft. His Zero squadron could sortie no more than two aircraft at any time. However even with limited air resources, the crafty fifty-seven year-old diehard was determined to let his enemies know that the Eleventh Air Fleet was still a force to be reckoned with.

The commanding officer of the formidably named 105th "paper" air force was Rear Admiral Eisho Saito, a 1914 graduate of the Naval Academy at Etajima.

Described as a gentle and kind hearted individual, Saito was not an air force man and had no experience in aviation matters. The task of running the Zero squadron fell to Commander Tomoyoshi Hori. He was formerly an executive officer of the 151st Air Group, a reconnaissance outfit. When his unit left for Truk in May 1944, he remained behind at the insistence of Admiral Kusaka. His administrative and organizational talents would have been hard to replace.

Commander Tomoyoshi Hori had arrived in Rabaul in August 1943. The enemy welcomed him to Rabaul three days after he landed by bombing his barracks and destroying his beloved Samurai sword, a treasured family heirloom.[2] The thirty-five year old 1930 Etajima graduate was aptly suited for the new task. He was a veteran pilot with over 4,500 flight hours in the Type 95 seaplane scout (single float biplane).

**Rear Adm. Eisho Saito  (Credit:  Takeshi Saito)**

**Comdr. Tomoyoshi Hori (Credit: Hori)**

"During the China War," he relates, "I had an experience to fight with an English fighter over Canton in early 1938. One day, I shot down an enemy scout plane over Canton and on the next day, we (four Type 95s) encountered an English Gloster Gladiator. The pilot was an Englishman, a lieutenant commander. We fought for over ten minutes, but the power of the enemy plane was too strong. The match ended in a draw. Before long, he gave up the fight and got away. When we returned to our carrier (*Kamui*), we found many bullet holes in our wings."[3]

In early 1941 before the outbreak of the Pacific War, Hori had been ordered to Thailand to serve as technical advisor to the Thai Navy. Thailand had purchased ten Type 95 scouts. Hori stayed on in Bangkok for over three months, training Thai pilots and acting as a test and ferry pilot. The Thai pilots and their instructors conversed in English, so Hori was obligated to sharpen his English language skills by intense study. After returning to Japan, he was decorated with the Fourth Order of the Crown from the Thai government.[4]

Commander Hori served in the Naval Aero-Technical Arsenal in Yokosuka as a test pilot from April 1941 until August 1943. He flew new prototypes and remodeled aircraft, exposing himself to inherent dangers on almost a daily basis.

There were only two serviceable Zeroes at Rabaul in June 1944 and over thirty fighter pilots. Most of the pilots were young, inexperienced, and sick with malaria. Many missions were given to Kawato and Shimbo, who stayed relatively healthy and volunteered for every operation.[5]

With the departure of Warrant Officer Shigeo Fukumoto in April, Ensign Chuhei Okubo would make a name for himself at Rabaul. On the opening day of the Pacific War, he had participated in the second wave attack on Pearl Harbor. He was a graduate of a navigator's course and was not a pilot. Okubo took over duties as ground officer and was the liaison between the top officers and enlisted pilots. When the 582nd Air Group (torpedo bomber unit) was withdrawn in February 1944, he remained behind.

Okubo was popular with the enlisted men. He was not a disciplinarian and was very flexible in his ways. Said his subordinate, Yoshinobu Ikeda, "Even though he outranked us, he was a good man and had plenty of guts! He was a great singer of Navy songs."[6]

The 105th Naval Base Air Unit, militarily speaking, was more of a construction unit than an air squadron. Of the approximately 4,000 men in the unit, roughly half were in the 101st and 212th Construction Corps. The 1,200 men in the aircraft maintenance section had virtually no aircraft to service. Everyone in the unit, including the pilots, helped dig caves and underground facilities to protect themselves and their supplies from bombing attacks.

Chuhei Okubo as a young navigator trainee, before the war. (Credit: K. Osuo)

Although their supply lines had been cut, Rabaul had more fuel than they could possibly use. They took their last delivery in November 1943. Aviation gas was all stored in fifty-five gallon steel drums, buried in holes and covered with four inches of soil.[7]

The biggest threat next to Allied bombardment was malaria. This disease, caused by single-celled parasite called plasmodia, are transmitted by the mosquito. The first symptoms include headache, nausea, and extreme weariness. This is usually followed by sudden chills and fever. Death by kidney and brain damage caused by malaria was quite common.

There was a major outbreak of malaria in May 1944. After mid-1944, supplies to Rabaul stopped and anti-malaria medicine (quinine) became nonexistent, along with other medical supplies. The last hospital ship Rabaul had seen was in January 1944.[8]

The medical staff and chemists at Rabaul were not about to surrender their health to the tropical menace of malaria. They searched New Britain unsuccessfully for the cinchona tree, which yielded the bark from which quinine was obtained. Botanists then searched for the cinchona's closest relative. The bark from the substitute tree was boiled into a stew and it was said to have provided some relief for malaria cases.[9] Still the illness increased dramatically and devastated whole units. About 95% of all personnel on Rabaul experienced at least one attack of malaria. This led to a decrease in food production because so many laborers were weakened.

The mosquitoes vied with the Allies for air supremacy in the tropical climate of New Britain and pretty much ruled the night. These nocturnal pests also brought forth dengue fever, which caused severe pain in the joints of its human victims, along with fever and rash.

Marine Corps PBJs plodding through Japanese flak over Rabaul. Crater Peninsula is at the bottom left. (Credit: USMC)

The Allied Forces bombarded their own island bases with DDT insecticide in a weekly spraying that was successful in preventing or reducing malaria cases. The Japanese on Rabaul did not have DDT, but did use a less effective insecticide called pyrethrum, burned mosquito coils and slept under netting, all without much success.

Those Japanese lucky enough to escape these debilitating diseases were usually plagued with athlete's foot. Dysentery (caused by contaminated water and lack of proper hygiene) was also very common, the victims suffering from abdominal cramps, fever, and diarrhea. Typhoid fever, respiratory infections, and blood diseases also contributed to the decline of Rabaul's garrison. Jungle rot was everywhere.

The Japanese Red Cross maintained a hospital in the mountains of Rabaul. Zero pilot Saburo Sakai recalls: "They were good, but supplies of medicine were inadequate. As far as military doctors, they were just as good as those in Japan."[10]

The overall morale of the Japanese Navy was quite good despite the harsh environment and the constant Allied bombardment. However, the pilots were a different breed. Trained to take the offensive, they were miserable about the lack of action. "From late 1944 through the end of the war, to tell you the truth, most of the Zero pilots lost their fighting spirit since there was no aerial combat, but just bombing with 60 kg bombs," Shibayama remembers.[11]

Rabaul was no paradise despite adequate food stocks and light duties. Being naval personnel, they had little thought of actual combat and believed the brunt of any fighting would be carried by their army counterparts.

Tobacco was cultivated and traded; the thin pages torn from pocket dictionaries and handbooks served as convenient cigarette paper. Officers and enlisted men shared a drag and commented on their miserable predicament while sharing thoughts of home.

Letters from home were a godsend, but as the war progressed, the US Submarine Service began taking its toll of supply ships plying the route between Rabaul and the homeland. Mail service became unreliable and stopped almost altogether by mid-1944.

Japanese and Korean "comfort girls" (prostitutes) provided entertainment for homesick men. Women of the 8th Consolation Unit were housed in downtown Rabaul. There were over 500 working girls brought over at the beginning of the war.[12] When General Kenney's Fifth Air Force began their savage bombing attacks against Rabaul in October 1943, the women were ordered out. They boarded transport ships for Japan via Truk, but many were sunk by submarines and very few ever saw their homeland again.

"There were hundreds of women for recreation," recalls Shibayama. "When I heard that they were going back to Japan, we gave them all of our money that we had at the barracks since we thought we were all going to die!"[13]

The Americans were very interested in one particular brothel and decided to put it out of business, although not for any moral reasons. Robert W. Griffith, who was a pilot in VMF-321, now of Ojai, California remembers:

"A coast watcher positioned near Rabaul was sending his natives into the town to work for the Japanese. They would return each night as there was a curfew forbidding natives to stay at night. They reported to him of a brothel for 'field grade' officers only in Rabaul. The exact location of the building and its activities were reported by the coast watcher to his superiors and it was decided that we should try to bomb the brothel at night when it was going full blast.

"We could not fly at night on Bougainville (this was before the PBJ squadron arrived) so an Army P-38 was flown to Bougainville to do the job.

"The P-38 made several practice flights to Rabaul to ascertain the correct location of the building and to await the full moon in order to get the best light. I have no idea whether the bombing was a success, but I doubt if it was ever known by more than a few people.[14]

"I have never seen a bomb attack at night by P-38 when I was at Rabaul," recalls Commander Tomoyoshi Hori. "In early 1944, B-25s sometimes bombed Rabaul at night. I think in those days, it was next to impossible for a few planes to bomb some specific target at night and hope for success. They would have needed a 'smart' missile of today."[15]

By the summer of 1944, Rabaul was completely isolated by Allied Forces. The Admiralty Islands had fallen the previous March, as well as Emirau to the east. Green Island had been taken in February. Both Emirau and Green Islands became important bases for the continued siege of Rabaul.

There were heated arguments at Rabaul HQ, senior staff officers believing that Green Island, 115 miles to their east, posed the greatest threat; they concentrated their meager air resources there. However, field officers were aghast that their headquarters had all but ignored the Admiralties. They held that the Admiralty Islands posed the greater threat.

Flight missions by Rabaul's Zero fighters were scrubbed for the entire two months of July and August, except for local training flights. On 15 September 1944, orders came down from headquarters to sortie two fighters on reconnaissance to the Admiralties.

Petty Officers Yasushi Shimbo and Masajiro Kawato, by reasons of health and experience, held a monopoly over flight missions. They volunteered and were accepted for the long range reconnaissance. The duo took off and maintained zero altitude, trying to evade enemy Corsairs that may have been lurking about. It was their luck that F4Us of VMF-115 and 211 were operating around Kavieng that day.[16]

Shimbo and Kawato arrived over Los Negros and spent the next 15 minutes counting the warships and aircraft from 12,000 feet. "There were two floating docks, six battleships (two of them in the dock under repairs), five carriers, and many cruisers and destroyers," observed Kawato.

Enemy aircraft! Shimbo suddenly dove and his wingman lost sight of him. Kawato also managed to successfully disengage, but diverted off course toward Emirau. He remembered there was an American airfield there and decided to pay them a courtesy call.[17]

The Americans on Emirau were hardly expecting any Japanese visitors. VMB-433 was celebrating its first anniversary and all operations were secured for the day. The enlisted men were engaged in a sports program while the officers held a party at their club.[18]

Suddenly, a lone Zero came out of nowhere at low altitude, sprayed the flight line, hit nothing, and vanished. Rabaul's 105th Naval Base Air Unit had had another of its rare moments.[19]

1. *Japanese Naval Aces and Fighter Units*, 164.
2. **Correspondence from Tomoyoshi Hori, 2 October 1992.**
3. **Ibid., 8 March 1993.**
4. **Ibid.**
5. **Ibid.**
6. **Correspondence from Yoshinobu Ikeda, 1993.**
7. *U.S.S.B.S.*,**Interrogation of Captain Toshio Asayama, Japanese Navy, 66.**
8. **Ibid., 33.**
9. **Ibid.**
10. **Interview with Saburo Sakai, Manhattan Beach, CA, 21 October 1990.**
11. **Correspondence with Sekizen Shibayama, 1992.**
12. *U.S.S.B.S.*, **35.**
13. **Correspondence with Sekizen Shibayama, 25 June 1994. According to Shibayama, the working girls were all Japanese and Korean and there were no Chinese amongst them. The women were divided into two groups: one for the Navy and another for the Army. "Happy Hour" for the Navy pilots was from 4 to 8 o'clock; the officers used the facilities from 8 o'clock to midnight. A good time could be had for about 20 yen and pilots received favored treatment because of their image and extreme generosity.**
14. **Correspondence with Robert W. Griffith, 11 October 1993.**
15. **Correspondence with Tomoyoshi Hori, 11 February 1994.**
16. **Aircraft Action Reports of VMF-115 and VMF-211 for 15 September 1944.**
17. *Zero Sen Rabaul Ni Ari.*
18. **War Diary of Marine Air Group 61, 15 September 1944.**
19. *Zero Sen Rabaul Ni Ari.* **This strafing attack was so minor, it was not even mentioned in the War Diaries of MAG 12 and 61, nor recorded elsewhere. Robert W. Griffith heard about this incident; he was in the operations dugout on Emirau at the time. Another of his comrades also heard of this attack. Kawato wrote about his role in 1956 and claimed ten aircraft set afire. His wingman, Yasushi Shimbo, doesn't remember . Commander Tomoyoshi Hori stated to me that Kawato never reported this lone strafing attack to him and is skeptical.**

**The Allied airfield on Emirau Island which Masajiro Kawato strafed on this way back to Rabaul, 15 Sep 1944. (Credit: National Archives)**

# 13

# THE FOOD SITUATION

Food and troop morale have always been closely associated, especially during wars. World War II spurred the advance of food technology by the United States. The Japanese military, on the other hand, was backwards in these regards and lived off the land.

Yet the Allied effort to strangle Rabaul by cutting off incoming supplies did little to starve the defenders into submission. There were no dire food shortages as far as the 105th Naval Base Air Unit was concerned. Men still enjoyed rice three times a day as late as 1945, although in smaller quantities than a year previously.[1]

The total obliteration of downtown Rabaul by the hellish bombing raid on 3 March 1944 caused food rations to be reduced. Commander Sumio Sano, the supply corps officer of the Southeastern Fleet, recalled: "Out of a total of approximately fifty tons of hardtack and canned goods store here, about twenty tons were lost."[2]

Fish was the staple food in the Japanese diet next to rice. There was a naval fishing unit at Rabaul. When Allied bombers sank most of the trawlers, the Japanese resorted to bombing schools of fish from the air. After each raid on Simpson Harbor, thousands of dead fish floated in. Unfortunately, the vast array of weirdly colored fish posed gastronomic dangers. Some men died eating poisonous varieties.

Simpson Harbor was infested with sharks. Lieutenant Minoru Shinohara of the 8th Submarine Base Unit remembers one disturbing incident: "My men hooked a huge shark and brought it up. We couldn't believe our luck! When we gutted the shark, a human arm slid out." Thoughts of a huge feast quickly evaporated. The disgusted men threw the man-eater back into the water.[3]

Petty Officer Sekizen Shibayama notes that fighter pilots received special attention. "In Rabaul, pilots were treated specially. We were provided with plenty of wine, tobacco, ice cream which was made in Rabaul, and so on. As far as food was concerned, we were satisfied."[4]

Commander Hori elaborates on the food situation:

"Since the stoppage of traffic between Rabaul and our home country, we had stockpiled about a month's supply of rice to be used in case of enemy attack. We stored the rice in drums and in caves and air raid trenches. The rice did not mildew, but there were many worms in it. We ate the rice with the worms. We also raised sweet potatoes and vegetables in large gardens and farms; we also bred chickens and pigs. Also, we produced daily necessities by the use of primary materials, even tobacco and palm wine. These products were never rich, but they were good enough for daily life."[5]

A certain species of wild bird produced a huge egg which was coveted. They would nest around the many hot springs in the Rabaul area, laying their eggs in the soil and parties of men would venture into the jungles to hunt for these eggs.[6]

The Japanese, master gardeners noted for their green thumb, were very proud of their large native gardens. Their main crop was the sweet potato. They also grew cabbage, eggplant, and cucumbers. The warm climate, abundance of water, and extremely fertile soil produced a bountiful harvest. This also attracted pests.

The main threat against food production came from the ravenous sweet potato bug. At night, they would march over the potato fields like an undulating carpet, leaving a totally denuded field in the morning. The Japanese fought back by making a moat around the field. As the army of insects were floundering in the water, fuel was added and set on fire.[7]

The Americans were the other pest and took a keen interest in the native gardens which were mostly tended by Korean laborers. They periodically dumped bombs to help cultivate the fields, leaving huge craters.

Typical meals taken by air unit members consisted of rice, soybean paste soup with vegetables, bits

Lt. Minoru Shinohara. (Credit: M. Fujita)

**Aerial photo showing bomb strikes (lower right) against Japanese gardens and living quarters near Tobera in 1944. Note craters (top and left) from previous attacks. (Credit: Bob Millington)**

and pieces of pork, chicken, or fish, pickled vegetables (tsukemono), sweet potatoes, and some canned goods.

There was a fair supply of local fruits and too many coconuts. In addition to its juice, the despised coconut also produced oil which was used to fry foods and make soap. Coconut meat was mixed with rice.

By 1945, the food supply had deteriorated and the variety became monotonous. Said Yoshinobu Ikeda, "From January 1945 until March 1946, it was sweet potato, coconuts, and some rice at every meal!"[8]

Each unit on the island was responsible for the raising and distribution of food to their own members. While the 105th was adequately fed, some other units were on the verge of starvation. Lieutenant Minoru Shinohara, a gunboat commander, remembers subsisting on "grass in salt soup" and sweet potatoes. Once, he took several drums of liquefied sugar and went around Rabaul, looking for a unit to trade with. It took him three days to make the transaction so he could bring food back to his men.[9]

Underground protection for foodstuffs was required by the constant air raids. The Japanese had already lost 500 tons of rice out of a total of 8,000 tons in April 1944. Rice was packed in sacks and stored under open air sheds and later stored in tunnels with dire con-

sequences. "It was a gamble to either put it in the tunnels and have it rot, or put it out in the open and have it destroyed by bombing," said Commander Sano. Much of the rice was lost to rotting.[10]

The damp atmosphere in the tunnels and caves also contributed to the spoilage of canned goods; they rusted. Losses from rotting was about thirty percent, and it was difficult to separate the good from the spoiled.[11]

Allied Forces also had their share of food problems, but it was one of quality rather than quantity. Fresh food was very scarce and meals came out of giant economy sized cans and boxes. Bob Millington, then a Marine captain in VMB-413 recalls:

"We had a good mess hall and kitchen at Stirling Island and elsewhere...I can't tell you too much about the breakfasts, because, for the most part, I skipped them. The ones I did partake of consisted of dehydrated eggs or as we said 'hydraulic' eggs as you had to add water, hot cakes, and we must have had syrup. Once in a great while, we would have canned bacon. The butter served at all meals, we referred to as 'axle grease.' It was canned and guaranteed not to melt at 100 degree temperature. It didn't!

Spam became a staple in the American military diet in WW II. The SW Pacific AAF fighter squadron unit designation was deleted by censors. (Credit: Geo. Hormel Co.)

"Our bread, which I don't ever remember being toasted, was made daily, was of very course texture, and was always full of weevils. Lieutenant Commander Robert A. (Al) Behrendt, our Squadron Flight Surgeon (who in the 1920s had been all-Coast or all-American end at USC) told us not to worry about the weevils; that cooking killed all germs, besides, they furnished us with protein. He said, 'just pretend you are eating raisin bread.'

"We had our share of Spam, which came in five pound cans. It was prepared in every conceivable way that Spam can be prepared - fried, stewed, SOS. We had more than our share of 'hydraulic' potatoes, beets, and carrots. These were the first dehydration undertaking of vegetables. The ingredients were diced in small cubes and none of it tasted fit to eat.

"Sunday meals were real jewels. This was the cooks day off and everything was served cold. We had cold Pork and Beans, cold canned tomatoes, cold Spam, sliced, weevily bread, and butter, with canned peaches for dessert...The coffee was usually pretty good."[12]

Of course, life in the chow lines would not be complete without an accompanying horror story, compliments of Bob Millington:

"Down at 'Maudie's Mansion' at Munda, we got a terrific load of frozen sheep liver from Australia. We had it at least once a day. The only explanation I have for it, is that we were at the end of the reverse 'lend-lease.' When the Navy picked up the meat in Australia, they, of course, took the chops; at New Caledonia, they took the hind legs; at Espiritu Santo, they took the forelegs; Guadalcanal got the rest of the carcass, except for the liver, and at Munda, we got more damn frozen sheep liver that I ever hope to see again. It was sort of green by the time it reached us...Fortunately, we had Ketchup and Cocktail Sauce, which helped to camouflage the liver!"[13]

Tom Blackburn, commanding officer of the Navy's famous "Jolly Rogers" (VF-17 Corsairs) had this to say about their chow:

"In November 1943 at Ondonga, New Georgia, we were based with the USAAF. We bunked in the large Quonset type huts and 'ate' in their officers' mess. The food was dreadful - ill conceived and ill prepared.

"In January - February on Bougainville, the VF pilots' camp was tri-service and the lodgings were canvas roofed 'cabins' – six pilots to a hut. Quite comfortable with a modicum of privacy. The pilots' mess was Navy staffed and operated and the chow comparable to a ship's wardroom."[14]

Royal New Zealand Air Force pilots were strangely satisfied with the American cuisine on Green Island. Says Bryan Cox of 16 Squadron: "Meals were good; we were introduced to such American delicacies as kernel corn, steak with pineapple and plenty of ice cream."[15]

The stress and strain of war caused men to drink or at least provided them with the excuse. With too much time on their hands, the defenders in Rabaul tried to make the best of it. Although sake (rice wine) was scarce, men improvised. Each unit had their own master brewer; juice from the buds of coconut trees were fermented to produce a powerful native brew (140 proof).[16] Booze production was officially sanctioned, unlike the American military. When not being bombed, idle Japanese bombed themselves with homemade rotgut.

"We always had sufficient beer, Coke, and whiskey," recounts Millington. "The officers took up a collection and bought 1,200 fifths of Schenley's 'Black Death,' which we shipped as "medical supplies" under a red cross. We only arrived with 900 fifths intact, as a case broke in the hold of the *Rotinin* or the *Mormac Wren*, and the Negro troops in the hold discovered it and consumed 300 fifths. The Navy wouldn't go into the hold to get them! We had tremendous quantities of canned grapefruit juice, which we used mainly as a mixer for our whiskey."[17]

Tom Blackburn:

"All booze was hard to come by, especially beer, and we put the arm on our flight surgeon, Lyle Herrmann for an inordinate amount of medical alcohol."[18]

1. **Preliminary P.O.W. Interrogation Report of Masajiro Kawato by Allied Translation and Interpreter Service(ATIS), 24 March 1945, Australian War Memorial, CRS A2663, File 779/3/37 II.**
2. *U.S.S.B.S.*, 68.
3. **Interview with Minoru (Shinohara) Fujita, Rosemead, CA, July 1992.**
4. **Correspondence with Sekizen Shibayama, 17 January 1992.**
5. **Correspondence with Tomoyoshi Hori, 15 January 1992.**
6. **Hori interview.**
7. **Ibid.**
8. **Correspondence with Yoshinobu Ikeda, 1992.**
9. **Fujita interview.**
10. *U.S.S.B.S.*, 69.
11. **Ibid.**
12. **Correspondence with Bob Millington, 18 September 1993.**
13. **Ibid.**
14. **Correspondence with Captain Tom Blackburn, 1993.**
15. **Correspondence with Bryan B. Cox, 1993.**
16. **Fujita interview.**
17. **Millington.**
18. **Blackburn.**

**This North American PBJ Mitchell of VMB-413 displays its lethal forward firing armament. A pair of fixed .50 caliber machine guns and one flexible .50 were mounted in the glass nose. Four more .50s were mounted in two side blisters of two each. When the top twin-.50 turret was aimed toward the nose the aircraft could employ nine forward firing guns. (Credit: Lambert)**

# 14

# GUIDED MISSILE ATTACKS AGAINST RABAUL

Wars have always played an important role in the development of weapons. It provided a real life testing ground for the introduction of new and sophisticated methods of mass destruction.

Unknown to most was the development of America's first successful combat-tested guided missile, the Interstate TDR, which had its origin within the Navy Bureau of Aeronautics. Prior to the beginning of World War II, the Navy was toying with the idea of utilizing drone aircraft primarily for fleet gunnery practice. However, imaginative minds came up with the concept of a "Kamikaze" bomber minus the pilot, and this had enough merit to warrant further exploration. The advent of an airborne TV camera/transmitter made the TDR assault drone a reality.

The TDR, a small twin-engined mid-wing monoplane aircraft, capable of carrying a 2,000 pound bomb, was manufactured by Interstate Aircraft and Engineering Corporation of El Segundo, California.[1] Because of its expendable nature, it was assembled using welded steel tubing and plastic skin. It was nothing more than an oversized, radio-controlled model airplane, with a wing span of forty-five feet and length of thirty. Two inexpensive 220 hp Lycoming engines provided power. Although it had a pilot's cockpit, it had been faired over for pilotless use. It could be launched from a catapult aboard ship or from an airstrip, and was guided to its target by a director aircraft. One hundred and eighty nine TDR-1s were manufactured at DeKalb, Illinois during 1943-44.[2]

The Japanese were also conducting parallel research on a radio-controlled aircraft. Commander Tomoyoshi Hori, executive officer of the 105th Naval Base Air Unit, played a leading part in the development and test flights of such aircraft.

"At the start, the Japanese Navy also made radio-control planes intended for use as targets in fleet gunnery exercises. The fact is, the Japanese Navy had accomplished two pilotless aircraft of sorts, in early 1942. At that time, I was serving at the Naval Aero-Technical Arsenal in Yokosuka as a test pilot.

"The outline of the method was that a real Type 94 Reconnaissance Seaplane (Allied codenamed Alf), equipped with a radio control equipment, was to be launched by catapult and fly under radio control from a director aircraft and make a safe water landing. That aircraft had safety equipment which enabled the pilot to change from 'automatic' to 'manual' during the test flight.

"During the test flight of these aircraft, I took off from the water by manual control, and once in the air, changed to automatic, and I released my hands and feet. When I felt danger, I would change to manual control. The result of the test flight was good at the beginning, but water landings brought many problems.

"In the Autumn of 1942, the final experiment (real pilotless) came into effect in Tokyo Bay. At the opening of the bay at Tateyama, we launched by catapult off the battleship *Yamashiro*. In advance, I was in the director aircraft. In the first test, the No.1 plane was launched, but just after release, its engine failed and it crashed into the sea. It was the first time failure! The second time, our No.2 aircraft launched successfully and I directed its flight around the mouth of Tokyo Bay for about thirty minutes, then turned it back and it made a suc-

The Interstate TDR was nothing more than an oversized radio controlled model aircraft. (Credit: National Archives)

cessful water landing near *Yamashiro*. The experiment was a success in spite of our first failure.

"At the time Japan was in war and the Japanese Navy did not have sufficient time and margin to produce a lot of such pilotless aircraft. I think now, if Japan had a lot of such equipment towards the end of the war, we might have achieved some successes in battle without having to resort to Tokko Tai (Kamikaze), the likes of a suicide mission!"[3]

The US Navy's Special Task Air Group One (STAG-1), arrived in the Russells (Sunlight Field, Banika Island, northwest of Guadalcanal) on 12 June 1944. Armed with the TDR and full of confidence, they put on a demonstration for Admiral E.L. Gunther (Commander Air Forces, South Pacific) and Major General Ralph Mitchell (USMC), Commander of the Air Forces for the Solomon Islands. Two out of four TDRs demolished a beached Japanese merchant hulk near the northwest tip of Guadalcanal. Admiral Gunther was impressed.[4]

Admiral William Halsey, commander of the South Pacific Area, believed that the new weapon had merit and should be tested under combat conditions. However, "battleship admirals" in Washington had their eyes on disbanding the unit. While Commodore Oscar Smith, head of STAG-1 went to Washington to battle the enemies of the TDR program, Commander Bob Jones (acting commander) took the equipment into combat operations.

On 27 September 1944, the TDR received its baptism of fire. Squadron VK-12 sortied four drones against Japanese ships anchored one mile southwest of Kahili Airfield on Southern Bougainville. Three TDRs scored two direct hits and a near miss and destroyed an anti-aircraft battery.

Mission Two occurred on 1 October when eight TDRs were launched against anti-aircraft positions on South Bougainville. According to the official report: "One

The Japanese Navy's first drone aircraft was the Type 94, but the program was scrapped as the war progressed. (Credit: K. Osuo)

hit was scored on a heavy position west of Ballale, and one on an automatic weapons position NE of Kangu. One TDR fell 300 ft. short of heavy guns south of Ballale, and two landed on Poporang Ridge. There were two duds in the target area, and one equipment failure, resulting in explosion in the air four miles north of Moila Pt."[5]

The initial attacks weren't spectacular, but there were high hopes. On 5 October, four TDRs were directed against Rabaul from their new base on Green (Nissan) Island. They were led to the target area by Grumman TBM Avengers (one TDR for each TBM). Two were lost due to technical problems and the remaining two exploded onshore, far from their targets.

An early TDR attack was witnessed by Commander Hori. His headquarters was located on the central highlands about nine miles east of Vunakanau Airfield. The highlands were near the coast, jutting more than 900 feet above the sea, with a commanding view of Simpson Harbor and Rabaul.

A TDR test flight over Half Moon Bay, Calif. in March 1944. A 2,000 lb. bomb is slung under the belly. (Credit: National Archives)

"I usually visited various sites by car," recalled Hori. "Once, our car was strafed by an enemy fighter and was destroyed by fire on the way to the airfield. At that time, I would visit the HQ in Rabaul Town by car, once or twice a month. Then I encountered the TDR attack on the way to HQ.

"Due to my experience, when I saw the first TDR attack at Rabaul, at once I could understand what it was. I remember that I saw its attack at Rabaul about seven or eight times. Each time, our force suffered lightly and we didn't feel any sense of danger."[6]

Naval Lieutenant Minoru Shinohara also witnessed the TDR attacks, but had a different reaction.

"It was a very small plane the first time I saw it. We wondered what it was. It made a small noise. Then I saw a larger plane at the entrance to the bay and realized that it was the director aircraft. We would hear the sound, and then all of a sudden, it would stop. We were scared because we had no idea where it was going to hit.[7]

"Our headquarters gathered the wreck of the TDR," continues Hori, "and we investigated it. I selected the minimum important parts from the wreckage. These materials were sent to Japan on November 8, 1944 by *Gekko* (twin-engined reconnaissance plane), but the plane went missing on the way to Truk."[8]

While Commander Hori poked through the wreckage to see what could be salvaged of the cockpit instruments, soldiers were busy trying to recover the engines' spark plug/generator assembly. When two wires were crossed, it produced a spark to light cigarettes; matches were scarce. They did have a "cigarette lighter" made from Zero engine parts, but they were very heavy and cumbersome. The TDR's engine parts were smaller and lighter.

As criticism mounted back in Washington, STAG-1 needed a spectacular success. It was decided to take out the causeway bridge linking Matupi Island to Rabaul in Simpson Harbor. This demanded pinpoint accuracy. On 9 October, VK-12 launched four TDRs. Two drones were shot down by heavy anti-aircraft fire, one crashing into the harbor one-quarter mile north of the bridge and the second one also came down in the water. The third TDR landed 100 yards from an anti-aircraft position and the fourth failed to reach the target. The advocates behind the TDR program were beginning to sweat. The purpose of the program was not to provide Japanese anti-aircraft gunners with convenient target practice.

It was "go for broke" on 15 October. Once again, the bridge was targeted for destruction. VK-11 was given the honors. According to the official report: "Of four TDRs, one crashed and sank midway between Duke of York and Cape Gazelle; one passed through the saddle,

over the bridge, circled for nine minutes, and crashed on the west side of the harbor; one exploded on the southwest side of Hospital Ridge; and one hit a secondary target area." The three misses were attributed to TV failures.[9]

Roger Newton, a radioman with STAG-1, recalls that the TDR was controlled by a joy stick, much like the control mechanism on today's TV video games, with a function dial. The television screen was green tinted and around five inches in diameter. A movie camera mounted behind the operator's shoulder filmed the small TV screen to record results.[10]

The last TDR attack was launched against Rabaul on 26 October. Two drones actually hit some buildings close to the intended target. The third went into the ocean at the southwest tip of Duke of York Island. The fourth TDR, diverted to Cape St. George, demolished a lighthouse.

A total of forty-two TDRs were launched against targets at Rabaul and Bougainville (nineteen against the former). The results were somewhat underwhelming. Strong radio interference en route to Rabaul by friendly forces caused some to fly erratically and miss their targets.

Commander Hori comments on the effectiveness of the TDR:

"The TDRs came and went and I don't believe their attacks were very effective. I thought they were just testing it. We didn't throw much flak at them, although when they came down to lower altitude, soldiers fired on them with machine guns and small arms. The mother plane was always way out there and we didn't bother to waste our ammunition on them." [11]

W. Raymond Woolrich, a pilot in STAG-1, remembers the Japanese commenting on their attacks at Rabaul: "It is reported that Tokyo Rose announced this strike as follows: 'The Americans are now using a flying box. It must be radio controlled for there is no pilot in them. We have just captured one of them.'"[12]

The official US Navy report was hardly enthusiastic: "Obviously, in its present stage of development, the assault drone is far less accurate and effective than the more ordinary bombing methods."[13]

On 27 October 1944, one day after their final assault on Rabaul, the Navy decommissioned STAG-1 and the assault drone program was terminated.

Captain Robert F. Jones USN (Ret.), now of Cape Canaveral, Florida, was quite proud of his unit's achievement: "As you know, our television aimed missile project was Top Secret and had powerful opposition. In '44, we made 46 attacks, had 45,6% direct hits. No KIA, no MIA, no POWs, no injuries. No loss of central aircraft."[14]

In 1966, Steve G. Simpson, then a journalist with the Times Courier of New Guinea, stumbled upon a wreckage of a TDR in the jungles of Rabaul. He was led to the site by a local native, who as a boy, had worked

A television screen in the mother aircraft dislays the approach of the TDR toward the experimental target ship off Guadalcanal. (Credit: Gary Nila)

The TDR is seen (above) just before it struck the target vessel, and (below) at the moment of successful impact. (Credit: Gary Nila)

as a mess servant at the Lakunai Airfield's pilot mess hall. Laying undisturbed about seventy-five yards away from the wreckage was the TDR's rusty bomb. Simpson took photographs of the wreckage and wrote letters to the US Air Force, inquiring about the strange aircraft. They initially professed no knowledge of any such aircraft. When Simpson returned to the crash site for further investigation, he was devastated. Fearing evil spirits, the natives had set fire to the wreckage and detonated the bomb; there was very little left.[15]

The only TDR in existence today is displayed at the Naval Aviation Museum in Pensacola, Florida. Today's ultra-sophisticated "smart" missiles can trace their ancestry directly to the crude but innovative Interstate TDR.

1. *Janes All World Aircraft*, 1947.
2. Kenneth Munson, *American Aircraft of World War II* Blandford Press, England, 1982, 94.
3. Correspondence from Tomoyoshi Hori, 1 March 1993.
4. Chronology of Special Air Task Force's Story, private writings of Captain Robert F. Jones (USN, Ret.), 1990, 12.
5. *Analysis of Pacific Air Operations*, October 1944, Serial 001883, 30 December 1944, Office of Naval Records and Library.
6. Correspondence from Tomoyoshi Hori, 1 May 1993.
7. Interview with Minoru Fujita, Rosemead, CA, 15 July 1993.
8. Hori.
9. *Analysis of Pacific Air Operations*, October 1944.
10. Telephone interview with Roger Newton, 24 October 1993.
11. Interview with Tomoyoshi Hori, Temple City, CA, 20 October 1993.
12. Correspondence from W. Raymond Woolrich Jr., 12 August 1993.
13. *U.S.S.B.S.*,.
14. Correspondence from Captain Robert F. Jones, 24 July 1993. Captain Jones also sent the author a videotape made from films taken off the television transmission of the TDR demonstration attack on the *Yamazuki Maru*, 30 July 1944. Films were also made of the Rabaul attacks and some former members of STAG-1 have them.
15. *Flypast*, September 1982, "The Flying Bombs of Rabaul," via David J. Duxbury, 3 April 1993.

# 15

# A UNIQUE ZERO FIGHTER IS BORN

Commander Tomoyoshi Hori was the man most closely associated with the development of Rabaul's novel two-seat Zero fighters. While the Navy did have a few A6M2-K tandem-seat trainers in Japan, none were ever shipped to Rabaul.

Admiral Kusaka, Captain Sanagi, and Commander Hori discussed the need for a fast reconnaissance aircraft. Single-seat Zeroes had been used, but their radio equipment was totally useless over long distances. Since they lacked aerial cameras, observations were made the old fashioned way - with eyeballs glued to binoculars. With an observer sitting behind the pilot in the Zero, intelligence data could be sent back to headquarters via a Morse code key transmitter immediately.

"The voice radio in the Zero was mainly used for communication among comrade planes or between plane and base on the ground," recalls Hori. "So I think its possible communication range was only five to ten kilometers. The Morse code key transmitter in the double-seat Zero had a range of over a thousand kilometers, so it was very easy to telegraph a report from the Admiralty Islands back to Rabaul."[1]

The first "production" of the two-seater occurred in the autumn of 1944, around October.[2] Remanufacturing was hampered by the lack of suitable hulks. These aircraft retained two nose-mounted 7.7mm machine guns and the 20mm wing cannon. Only two such aircraft would ever be built. It was not a major engineering feat; a space for the observer's seat and telegraphic equipment were added behind the pilot's compartment. Commander Hori personally ground tested the aircraft's communication equipment and found it satisfactory

On 15 October 1944, Masajiro Kawato and Fumio Wako took off for a recon of the Admiralties. The pair of Zeroes (the two-seater version was not in use at this time) arrived over the islands around 1500 hours. Kawato proceeded to record his observations:

"Two or three small navy craft in each floating dock, five or six damaged aircraft carriers and cruisers and several other small craft...[3] About thirty minutes later I saw a group of F4U's over Kabien."[4]

They may have spotted VMF-115 returning from Guadalcanal after picking up new Corsair aircraft. The Americans reported no contact with enemy aircraft and the Zeroes returned to Vunakanau without mishap.

When the two-seater Zero was available for duty, Petty Officer Masajiro Kawato was relegated to flying the new aircraft, but the reasons for this are not entirely clear. According to Sekizen Shibayama, "Kawato was banned to fly single; instead, he flew with a fellow (instructor) in two-seat Zero used for training because he was considered unstable in mind."[6]

Kawato's reckless demeanor and past history of losing Imperial property was a matter of record (he had lost three Zeroes in three months). He had a reputation as a hothead, and in the new aircraft, a senior pilot or observer could keep an eye on him. However, Commander Hori believes differently: "I think the reason why Kawato only flew the double-seat Zero was not because of his unfitness for single-seat Zeroes, but because of his fitness for double-seat Zeroes."[7]

By the beginning of November 1944, Admiral Kusaka and his staff decided that a morale booster was needed. He looked toward the Admiralties. Successful recon missions to the Admiralties on 15 and 19 October, and another on 1 November indicated that enemy radar and combat air patrols were not a serious threat. If Allied commanders thought that Rabaul had lost its sting, Kusaka was prepared to strike.

**1. Interview with Tomoyoshi Hori, Temple City, CA 20 October 1993.**
**2. Masajiro Kawato reported in his memoir that he test flew one of the two-seat Zeroes in March 1944 and shot down a twin-engined bomber over Simpson Harbor along with three other pilots. He further wrote that Rear Admiral Saito and his staff witnessed this combat. His account is incorrect; the two-seater did not exist at this time and Rear Admiral Saito was not connected to the Zero squadron until June 1944.Squadron Leader D.S. Hamilton's Interrogation of Japanese Aircrew says five twin-seat Zeroes were made! But Commander Hori insists that there were only two. Hamilton's report contains errors due to guessing and misunderstanding by the Japanese. The Zero squadron did not have radio operators for the back seat until Hori brought them over from the seaplane 958 Air Group after the 105th was established in June 1944. Hori stated that the first production aircraft was completed just before the 9 November 1944 bombing attack on Momote Airstrip.**
**3.** *Zero-Sen Rabaul Ni Ari.*
**4. Ibid. Kawato writes that he and his wingman saw a group of 24 F4F (Wildcats) over Kavieng on their way back to base. In 1978, a ghostwriter translated Kawato's original 1956 memoir, Zero-Sen Rabaul Ni Ari, into Flight Into Conquest, which was later retitled Bye Bye Blacksheep. Surprisingly, there is not one reference to an F4U in his original work; the F4Fs were changed to F4Us in Kawato's American edition.**

5. War Diaries of VMF-115 and 211 for 15 October 1944. They were operating on Emirau during this time; both units moved to Leyte (Philippines) in December. 1944. They patrolled and attacked Japanese positions around Kavieng (New Ireland) and New Hanover. Kawato writes that the enemy fighters followed them from Kavieng to Rabaul. Kawato's version is not supported by American military records.

6. Correspondence from Sekizen Shibayama, 26 November 1991.

7. Correspondence from Tomoyoshi Hori, 8 September 1992.

Type 98 reflector guns (right) were the standard equipment on Zeroes. The graduated ring and bed sight (in down position) was popped up between the glass lens if the imaging light bulb was burned out. It was crude in comparison to American computerized gunsights, but it was effective. (Sakaida)

A Tokyo museum view of a two-seat A6M2, Model 21. The tail code indicates that this aircraft was assigned to the 253rd Air Group on Rabaul. (Credit: Kazuhiko Osuo)

# 16

# RABAUL STRIKES BACK

Reconnaissance sorties to the Admiralties had convinced Admiral Kusaka that there were targets worth going after. The date selected was 9 November 1944. Ensign Chuhei Okubo was given the assignment of bombing suitable targets on Los Negros Island. Rabaul was going to send its entire air force to do the job – two regular Zero fighters and their newest two-seater version.

Mechanics wheeled out 60 kg incendiary cluster bombs and attached one under each wing. Two bombs were the most that could be carried by each plane. Each bomb consisted of forty sticks and were designed to break open after a certain length of fall. With this "shotgun" bombing technique, they were bound to hit something.

The flight was briefed by Commander Hori to minimize the danger to their precious aircraft. "Don't fly

FO Hugh Kennare beside his Spitfire Mark VIII of 79 Squadron RAAF. (Credit: H. Kennare)

any lower than 12,000!" Hori warned. "Take a good look, select your targets, drop your bombs, and get out quickly." The assault team saluted smartly and ran for their aircraft.[1]

Okubo jumped into the back of the two-seat Zero, and Masajiro Kawato took the pilot's position. Petty Officers Fumio Wako and Yasushi Shimbo boarded their single seat aircraft. At 1320, the three Zeroes roared off from the dusty airstrip at Vunakanau as Admiral Kusaka, his staff, and the entire air base personnel cheered them on.[2]

Momote Airstrip on Los Negros Island, far removed from the battle lines, was deadly dull duty for the pilots of 79 Squadron RAAF. Flying Officer Hugh Kennare was one of two pilots from the unit who were on readiness patrol that day in early model Spitfires. He remarks:

"By September, 79 Squadron's pilots were aware that new Mark VIII Spitfires were waiting for them at an aircraft depot in Queensland. They became frustrated by the fact that Momote was removed from front line operations and that they could not take possession of their new Spitfires and join up with two similarly equipped squadrons (Nos. 452 and 457) in operations over the Halmahera Islands. Only two aircraft were being kept 'at readiness' from dawn until dark. The Squadron was in a back-water, away from the real war; a situation not conducive to good morale."[3]

Flying Officer Kennare had been given permission to take-off for an hour of practice flight. The weather was excellent, and he looked forward to the possibility of challenging American F6F Hellcat pilots in mock dogfights.

"I spent about forty-five minutes stalking such aircraft from up-sun positions, and then diving through the scattered clouds to make simulated attacks on them," he recalls. "I remember diving towards an Army Air Force Black Widow nightfighter and finding that the crew members were very alert to my intentions. The pilot turned his aircraft steeply and hard towards me at the right moment and foiled my 'attack.' He was no amateur and probably knew a lot more than I did!"[4]

Meanwhile, the three intruders were flying toward the Admiralties in a straight line course at 18 - 20,000 feet. No. 334 RS (radar station) detected some-

The crew of No. 337 Radar Station who detected the approach of the three Japanese raiders on 9 Nov 44. (Credit: Ed Simmonds)

thing strange on their scope at Cape Gloucester on the western tip of New Britain, but no warning was issued. Station No. 337, located at the southern end of Momote Strip, detected three aircraft at eighty miles, bearing 113 degrees, received no IFF (a transponder called Identify Friend or Foe) and tracked them to fifteen miles. Movement Control reported the three bogies as "friendlies".[5]

Admiral Kusaka and his staff knew that radar would eventually spot the approaching attack force, but were betting that their aircraft would be mistaken for friendlies, and had guessed correctly. The Allies believed that Rabaul no longer had any aircraft, hence, an aerial assault from that quarter was unimaginable.

"I returned to Momote Airfield, landed and taxied to the readiness point close to the runway," remembers Kennare. It had been a good practice flight. "The ground crew refueled my Spitfire immediately and plugged in a battery cart for restarting the engine. My flying helmet, oxygen mask and gloves were draped over the control column. The refueling tanker was still standing in front of the airplane and I was standing by the wing root and cockpit, still wearing my life-jacket and other escape gear, and talking with the ground crew when the first cannon shells from the raiding Zeros began exploding."[6]

The Japanese raiders arrived over Hyane Harbor on Los Negros Island unchallenged. There were a dazzling array of targets: a large aviation supply depot, overhaul and repair shops, a pontoon assembly depot, repair and fuel piers, warehouses, buildings, and cranes. Momote Strip had USAAF and RAAF aircraft parked close together. With so many choices, very little time, and six cluster bombs, they could not hope to inflict any significant damage. Their assault would be nothing more than an insult.

A group of approximately seventy parked aircraft caught Okubo's eye. "That's it! Get the aircraft!" shouted Okubo to the pilot. The ensign ordered Kawato down to 6,000 feet. As Kawato dove, he opened up with his guns as the other two planes followed. They could see men scattering in all directions below.

Kawato lobbed one bomb towards the airfield but the other failed to come off the bomb rack. He pulled up sharply at around 4,500 feet and the second bomb tore away. Accuracy suffered.[7]

"Momentarily, we were completely puzzled by what was happening, but then the high pitched sound of the Zeroes pulling out of their dives caught our attention and I looked up to see one of them overhead," remembers Kennare. "I caught a fleeting glimpse of a sec-

Momote Airstrip, Los Negros Island in the Admiralties in 1944, with over 100 aircraft visible. (Credit: Ed Shanley)

ond Zero, but in a flash they had gone in an easterly direction. The raid was over before we realized fully what had happened.[8]

"I 'guestimated' that neither aircraft had descended below four or five thousand feet in its dive. They certainly did not press home their attack as they easily could have done, especially with Momote's defences caught completely off guard. I think those Japanese pilots must have laughed all the way back to Rabaul."[9] Aviation Machinist Mate Third Class Edward J. Shanley was working on aircraft as a member of Aviation Repair and Overhaul Unit No.1 when the attack began.

"I was on the make-ready line," the sixty-eight year old vet from Dracut, Massachusetts remembers. "One came right up the strip – bang, bang, bang, and he kept on going. It was over before it got started! We ran for cover. There was no anti-aircraft guns because they had been moved out in preparation for the Philippines invasion."[10]

As the three Zeroes were hightailing it home, a B-24 was spotted about ten miles south of Momote. The Liberator was flying at around 5,000 feet and the Japanese were at 6,000. Kawato wanted to attack it, but Okubo, not wanting to push their luck, nixed the idea and ordered him to stay on course. The Zeroes and the

bomber passed about a thousand yards apart, the bomber making no sign that it had seen them.[11]

As the raiders were racing for home, two Spitfires roared off after them, but precious time had been lost. "My first impulse was to 'scramble' immediately without Flight Lieutenant O'Dea who was in the Operations Room, more than 200 meters away," says Kennare. "However, I had been reprimanded by my Commanding Officer for doing exactly that on a previous occasion and, therefore, waited for O'Dea to reach his aircraft and start the engine...The Japanese pilots headed for Rabaul at high speed and we had no chance of overtaking them, even with our engines giving full power."[12]

"We destroyed over thirty enemy aircraft on the ground!" reported Ensign Okubo upon landing. The news spread like wildfire. For the more than 36,000 Navy men stationed at Rabaul, this was the best news in months. Morale soared to Alpine heights and even the Army was impressed.

Rabaul HQ reported the results of their daring attack to Imperial Headquarters in Tokyo. The next day, the air unit received a congratulatory "well done!" message. The official proclamation read: "Our air force unit, on the afternoon of November 9th, attacked the enemy airfield in the Admiralty Islands. Setting fires in bombing attacks on eight sites, we destroyed on the ground thirty of fifty large and medium aircraft."[13] In keeping with tradition, there were no citations, commendations, or medals issued to the individuals involved not even a feast.

The war diary of the US Naval base described the results in far different terms:

"On 9 November at approximately 1505, three Japanese planes came over Momote Strip at high altitude, dropping approximately thirty 1-kilogram anti-personnel bombs and strafing the strip with 20-mm explosive bullets. The damage was very slight. A gas tank was demolished; the mail storage tent and the BATU Snack Bar were hit. Two planes on the ground were holed. Eight men were injured; none seriously. The planes apparently came from Rabaul, circling around Kavieng, and coming in on the transport lane. They were picked up on radar, but not identified as unfriendly until they opened fire. Two of our planes took off in pursuit, but were unable to make contact with the enemy."[14]

Upon returning to Momote, Kennare and O'Dea spoke to the controller via telephone about their failure to detect the intruders by radar. In the conversation that followed, it was learned that the Zeroes detected fifteen minutes before Kennare had first landed, were mistaken for three US Navy Corsairs being ferried to the Admiralties along the correct route for such flights. It was assumed that the Americans had failed to switch on their IFF.

Dr. Hugh Kennare, now recently retired from the position of Chief Executive Officer of the South Australian Dental Service, comments further:

"Two impressions of the incident remain clear in my mind. First, my admiration for the navigational skill of the Zero pilots in successfully making the trip from Rabaul to Momote, and apparently back to Rabaul safely without an escort, and for their daring to attack such a formidable target. The odds should have been against them, but they obviously knew of the value of surprise - one of the ten cardinal principles of war...Second, I remember my frustration with the Controller who saw no reason to direct me to a position to intercept the Zeros, especially as I was already in a good position to do so."[15]

The sneak attack on Momote caused great consternation on nearby Emirau Island and an immediate punitive raid against the Japanese in the Kavieng area was quickly planned. Captain Bob Millington of VMB-423 helped the duty officer arouse the PBJ crews out of their bunks but unfortunately, foul weather foiled the plans. Millington recalls:

"The mission was canceled the next morning because of weather after the loss of two SBDs shortly after take-off. I had a hell of a time shaking drunks out of the sack at that hour. The reception I got was highly unmilitary. They couldn't fathom the Jap attack or the need to strike back. We were unsure of where the Zeroes came from."[16]

The Japanese paid dearly for their audacious attack. "The following day, and for the next ten days, between fifty and sixty B-24s raided us," Kawato remembered. "They bombed the rubber forest where our aircraft were hidden, and we lost two of our precious planes."[17]

As a direct result of the successful Japanese attack on Momote Airstrip, No.23 Squadron, RNZAF, sent up a squadron of F4U-1 Corsairs from Piva Strip (Bougainville) to Mokerang Airstrip on Los Negros Island. They began patrolling the area from November 23rd (dawn and dusk patrols). Having been burned once the Allies vowed not to let it happen again.

1. Correspondence from Tomoyoshi Hori, 1993. Also *Zero-Sen Rabaul Ni Ari*.
2. *Rabaul Sen Sen Ijo Nashi*.
3. Correspondence from Hugh D. Kennare, 11 September 1992.
4. Ibid.
5. Correspondence from Ed Simmonds, 19 October 1992.
6. Kennare.
7. *Zero-Sen Rabaul Ni Ari*.
8. Kennare
9. Ibid.
10. Telephone conversation with Edward J. Shanley, 10 March 1993.
11. Interrogation of Japanese Aircrew.
12. Kennare
13. *Saigo No Rabaul Zero-Sen Tai*, Kito Seiri. Also, *Rabaul Sen Sen Ijo Nashi*.
14. War Diary of Naval Base, Navy 3205, November 1944.
15. Kennare.
16. Correspondence from Bob Millington, 1994.
17. *Zero-Sen Rabaul Ni Ari*.

**RNZAF Corsairs (above) operated from Bouganville and Green Island against Rabaul and other Japanese bases. (Credit: B.B. Cox)**

**A RNZAF PV-1 Ventura (below) on patrol over Simpson Harbor in 1945. (Credit: B.B. Cox)**

# 17

# A BLACK DAY FOR THE KIWIS

There was very little activity for the Zero pilots in December, but they managed to lose more of their precious Zeroes. One aircraft was destroyed on 1 December when an Allied twin-engined bomber dropped a load on a rubber plantation near Vunakanau. It was carefully hidden, but a lucky hit demolished it.[1]

The continued air offensive against the Japanese in the Kavieng area of New Ireland was handed over to the Royal New Zealand Air Force on 1 December 1944. The three American Corsair squadrons based on Emirau Island (VMF-115, 211, and 313) packed up their gear and headed for the killing fields of Leyte (Philippines). No. 19 Squadron RNZAF inherited the fighter defense of Emirau and flew combat air patrols to Kavieng. Dawn and dusk patrols were the norm and two aircraft were kept on scramble alert at all times.[2]

The Kiwi air patrols served to remind the Japanese that the Allied Forces were still prosecuting the war even though Rabaul and Kavieng had been bypassed. There were three sorties by two aircraft daily and each F4U carried a 1,000 pound bomb to be dropped anywhere at the pilots' discretion. When there were enough planes available, up to eight were scrambled to attack targets of opportunity.

The New Zealanders, at Rabaul's "front door", took over duties from the remaining American Corsair squadron on Green Island. VMF-218 had left for the Philippines in November, and VMF-222 departed in mid-January 1945 joining the exodus. No. 18 Squadron RNZAF Corsairs maintained a standing patrol over the Rabaul Airfields. "Black Cats" (Catalina PBY flying boats) and Marine PBJs of VMB-423 also stayed on to harass the Japanese, along with the New Zealand PV-1 Venturas.

The constant patrols and bombing missions to Rabaul produced some casualties. Most were operational losses while others simply disappeared without a trace. First Lieutenant Moszek Zanger was one of the unlucky ones who lived long enough to tell his story.

On 5 December 1944, Zanger failed to return from a mission to Rabaul. He was last seen bailing out of his F4U at 1431, about two miles inland from Ataliklikun Bay. He was captured shortly afterwards and detained at Tobera Airfield.[3] When word of his capture reached the Zero pilots, he received some visitors. Petty Officers Yoshinobu Ikeda and Masajiro Kawato came to chat with the Polish born New Yorker. The exchanges were friendly and it was difficult for the Japanese pilots

to imagine that Zanger and his comrades were the cause of most of their misery.[4]

The Japanese Combined Fleet ordered a reconnaissance mission to scout the Admiralties again on 20 December and two planes were dispatched. Bad weather forced them to abort and the scouts returned empty-handed. The following day, a single Zero was sent aloft, was detected by patrolling F4Us, but managed to elude them and complete its mission. During landing, the undercarriage collapsed and the aircraft suffered major damage.[5]

New Year 1945 brought further misfortune. On 9 January 1945 veteran pilot, Chief Petty Officer Tokushige Yoshizawa failed to return from a mission to the Admiralties. Commander Hori believes that he had lost his bearing on his return flight and ditched in the sea.[6]

**CPO Tokushige Yoshizawa. (Credit: Y. Izawa)**

One of Rabaul's rare two-seat Zero aircraft on display in a Tokyo museum. Ditched by its crew, it was recovered by an Australian team near Cape Lambert in 1972. (Credit: Maru)

On 10 January, a single Zero was sent aloft to scout the Admiralties. It reportedly ran into a patrol of F4U Corsairs and skillfully evaded them. Masajiro Kawato accomplished his mission and returned.[7]

On 12 January 1945 Pilot Officer Harold P. Crump and Flight Sergeant Ronald R. Mitchell of 14 Squadron RNZAF spotted what they believed was a possible Val dive bomber over Cape Lambert at 1500 hours and gave chase. Crump's windscreen became streaked with oil, fouled his vision, and he was forced to delay his attack. Mitchell, who had first spotted the Japanese at 2,000 feet, tried to maneuver for the kill. The enemy pilot skillfully dove under him into clouds, then dropped his belly tank which exploded upon hitting the water. No shots were exchanged and this Japanese failed to become a RNZAF statistic.[8]

According to Japanese officer interrogations, they had no Vals on 12 January, and the lead Corsair engaged a Zero six miles east of Cape Lambert and the Japanese shot him down. The same officers believed that the Zero could have been a two-seater. The second Corsair then hit the Zero in the engine and it ditched in the sea. The pilot swam ashore and wandered in the jungle until rescued on 20 January.[9] Some Japanese believe that this pilot was Petty Officer Kentaro Miyagoshi, but others disagree.

An attempt was made to credit Pilot Officer Harold P. Crump with a victory, but being an honest sort, he would have none of it. Thus, the Royal New Zealand Air Force did not break the century mark and would eventually end the war with ninety-nine aerial victories.

In August 1972, two aircraft enthusiasts from Australia, Geoff Pentland and Barry Coran, recovered one of Rabaul's two-seat Zeroes from twenty-five feet of water at Cape Lambert. It was initially believed that this Zero belonged to Tokushige Yoshizawa. Human remains were reportedly found in the cockpit, but this was questionable. Some experts were not entirely con-

vinced that they were indeed human remains. The aircraft was later refurbished and sold and is now on display at the Tokyo Scientific Museum.

The mystery of the two-seat Zero may now be solved. Commander Hori believes that at that time, the second of Rabaul's only pair of twin-seaters had not been completed yet. He further explained that had there been a two-seater, then it would have been used for flights on the 9th and 10th, which involved only single-seat aircraft. They lacked communication equipment. Intelligence data had to be brought back by the pilot, whereas it could be telegraphed back to headquarters in the two-seater via a Morse code key transmitter.

Commander Hori believes that he has the answer to this unsolved mystery:

"I recalled that the double-seat Zero did not fly to the Admiralties. At the same time, I recalled a Zero flew to Turub (near the west end of New Britain and 460 km from Rabaul) for the mission of scouting the enemy troops which landed there. I think this case perhaps was that of the two-seat Zero in question. I think it was near the war's end...So I think it was after April 1945 and maybe some day in May or June."[10]

Commander Hori may be right. He remembers receiving a telegraphic message from the double-seater, saying that they were out of fuel and ditching on the sea near Cape Lambert. He also remembered the two crewmen returning to base through the jungles.[11]

Yoshinobu Ikeda recalls that in his chats with Kentaro Miyagoshi, his buddy recalled the harrowing experience in the jungles.

"He never mentioned being shot down over Cape Lambert," writes Ikeda. "He told me that he was shot down in a dogfight and parachuted down into the jungle where his parachute became caught on a huge tree. He had difficulty getting down. Then, he wandered around and

**PO Kentaro Miyagoshi**

tried to eat ants from ant hills, but it was difficult because he had problems with his mouth. He slept in trees at night. He was finally rescued and came back to the unit."[12]

Miyagoshi returned to the homeland in March 1945 by flying boat.

The interrogation report of the Japanese officers contains errors, probably due to answering without the benefit of documentation. They insisted that there was no flight on 12 January 1945, but there was and a Zero was lost, but the circumstances are unknown. Miyagoshi may have flown on the 12th, encountered the two Kiwi Corsairs, bailed out, and came up with a good story to tell his superiors.

The blackest day in Royal New Zealand Air Force history materialized on 15 January 1945. Three squadrons of F4Us (Nos. 14, 16, and 24), 36 aircraft in all, converged on Toboi Wharf on the outskirts of Rabaul Township. They began a bombing attack at 0900. Anti-aircraft fire was heavy and about fifteen minutes into the assault, the Japanese scored a hit on one aircraft. Flight Lieutenant Frank Keefe bailed out of his mount and floated down into the middle of Simpson Harbor in a hail of machine gun and small arms fire. The pilot discarded his dinghy and immediately swam for the harbor entrance.[13]

The Corsairs tried to protect their downed comrade by strafing the shoreline gun batteries. A US Navy Catalina PBY-5A flying boat of VP-44, piloted by Leland E. Dobberstein, circled the harbor, requesting permission to land and pick up Keefe. Mission commander, Squadron Leader Paul Green, surveyed the situation and denied permission. Unwilling to take no for an answer, Dobberstein took matters into his own hand and made an attempt anyway, escorted by two fighters. Murderous machine gun fire finally convinced him that a rescue attempt was, indeed, impossible.[14]

Undeterred, Keefe continued to swim against the powerful currents. After treading water for nearly nine hours, he was exhausted and clung to a log. At

1730, a rescue group of a dozen Corsairs and a Ventura, took off from Green Island. When they arrived over the harbor, the fighters began strafing the shoreline again while the PV-1 flew low. It dropped two rafts to Keefe, but he never made any attempt to retrieve them. Badly wounded, Keefe was captured by the Japanese and died on Rabaul.

There was nothing more to be done, so the New Zealanders reluctantly departed, not knowing that a violent storm was brewing between them and base. The pilots became disoriented in the hellish thunderstorm with zero visibility, and seven more brave airmen failed to return.[15]

1. **Interrogation of Japanese Aircrew. This may have been one of the two Zeroes destroyed or badly damaged by punitive strikes in retaliation for the 9 November 1944 bombing attack on Momote Airstrip. According to *Zero-Sen Rabaul*, Ni Ari, Kawato states that he and Yoshinobu Ikeda flew a recon mission to the Admiralties on 5 December 1944 in two separate aircraft. The official flight logs do not list this sortie, but the records are incomplete. Kawato does not describe this aircraft as a two-seater. Thus, it is quite possible that the two-seater was damaged and undergoing repairs at this time.**
2. **Royal New Zealand Air Force, 267.**
3. **USMC Casualty Report, 19 December 1945, Cas. No. 077083.**

**Flt. Sgt. Bryan Cox of 16 Sq., RNZAF, was part of the Keefe rescue mission and narrowly survived the killer weather front. (Credit: B.B. Cox)**

4. Masajiro Kawato stated to his interrogator that a First Lieutenant Zanga (sic) was captured and living with Japanese officers at Tobera. Yoshinobu Ikeda stated in letters to the author (28 March and 19 May 1994) that he had met Lieutenant Zanger at Tobera. According to his casualty card, Zanger was shot trying to escape and was buried. His remains were recovered and interred in a private cemetery in California. Mr. Ikeda was unaware of Zanger's fate and asked the author to help locate him. He was saddened to learn that Zanger had been killed.

5. *Saigo No Rabaul Zero-Sen Tai Kito Seiri.*

6. Correspondence from Tomoyoshi Hori, 16 February 1992.

7. *Zero-Sen Rabaul Ni Ari.* Kawato writes that he flew a reconnaissance mission to the Admiralties on this date, but was forced to abort due to bad weather. But according to *Saigo No Rabaul Zero-Sen Tai Kito Seiri,* the Zero ran into a patrol of F4Us.

8. Correspondence from David J. Duxbury, 20 March 1992, based upon COMZEAIRTAF signal to Air Department, dated 3 October 1945.

9. Interrogation of Japanese Aircrew.

10. Correspondence from Tomoyoshi Hori, 30 October 1992. Turub or Tsurubu was the Japanese name for Cape Gloucester.

11. Ibid., 8 October 1992.

12. Correspondence from Yoshinobu Ikeda, 1992.

13. Henry Sakaida, *Pacific Air Combat WWII - Voices From The Past*, Phalanx Publishing, St. Paul, MN, 1993, 52-53.

14. Bryan B. Cox, Pacific Scrapbook (private photo memoir, unpublished), New Zealand. Mr. Cox flew on the Keefe rescue mission and was the last Kiwi to see him alive.

15. Ibid. Disoriented in bad weather, Cox would have become a casualty, but a bolt of lightning saved his life; it illuminated the coastline of Green Island and he was able to land safely, celebrating his 20th birthday that day. For a more detailed account of this incredible rescue mission, see his book, *Too Young To Die - The Story of a New Zealand Fighter Pilot in the Pacific War*, Century Hutchinson, 1987

VMB-413 Mitchells hitting Vunakanau AD on 5 Jan 45. (Credit: Bob Millington)

# 18

# DUEL OFF CAPE ORFORD

The 108th Aircraft "Chop Shop" cranked out two "new" additions for Commander Hori at the end of February 1945, a pair of Nakajima B5N2, Type 97 (Kates). These single-engined torpedo bombers carried a crew of three and had a top speed of 235 mph at 11,810 feet.

Commander Hori did not have regular torpedo bomber crews for these Kates amongst the men in his unit, so he brought over two pilots and three observers from the 958th Air Group to train them. In the Japanese Navy, observers were also trained radiomen.[1]

Ensign Tokuya Takahashi was one of the two pilots of the Kates. He had joined the Navy in 1936 and commenced operations in February 1942 aboard an aircraft carrier sailing for Rabaul. An accomplished pilot with close to 2,600 flight hours, he had mixed feelings about his aircraft in 1945: "It was very safe to fly, good on take-off and landing, stalling and spinning, but it was too old and slow to be well liked."[2]

Local training flights were conducted about once a week and consisted of torpedo practice and landings. Night flights were made on the average of twice a month during full moon and consisted entirely of flying circuits and landings.

American night hecklers never gave them peace. Twice in March and April, the Kates were forced to abort their training when intruders were detected lurking in the area. The flare path was extinguished and the torpedo planes flew wide circles at 6,000 feet until the raider completed its task and departed.

The critical need for pilots in the home defense began to deplete the remaining ranks of Rabaul's guerrilla air force. When an Emily flying boat visited briefly on 3 March 1945, Petty Officers Yoshinobu Ikeda, Takashi Kaneko, Fumio Wako, and Kentaro Miyagoshi received their transfer orders. The lucky four boarded the aircraft and left the island hell hole. Kaneko was killed in action against B-29s over Kyushu on 29 April 1945, but the others would survive the war.[3]

In addition to enlisted pilots, veteran officers were desperately needed in the home defense. Commander Hori recalls: "I had also been ordered in early 1945 to return to Japan with a naval staff and seven Army generals by flying boat. We waited three times during a full moon night (once a month) for its landing at Rabaul, but the plane couldn't land due to the enemy's bombing attack and bad weather." Hori missed the boat.[4]

By 9 March 1945 there were only three serviceable fighters left. Of the eight Zero pilots who had flown since March 1944, four were disabled.[5] Yasushi Shimbo and Masajiro Kawato were ordered to sortie again. Their mission was to attack enemy ground forces surrounding their troops at Zungen, fifty miles south of Rabaul (Wide Bay area). Mechanics attached 70 kg incendiary

Some of Rabaul's contingent of remaining pilots in January 1945. L. to R., front row: Yoshio Sakamoto (958th), Yoshinobu Ikeda, Sekizen Shibayama, Jiro Nagai and Katsushi Hara (958th). Standing: Nobuo Miwata, Takashi Kaneko, Masajiro Kawato, Kingo Seo, Minamigawa, Shigeo Terao (958th), Isao Kochi, Fumio Wako and Toshikazu Umezu (958th). (Credit: Y. Ikeda)

**Tokio Shimizu just before joining the Navy. (Credit: Shimizu Family)**

clusters under each wing. Petty Officer Second Class Tokio Shimizu was selected by Ensign Okubo, in consultation with Shimbo, to accompany Kawato in the rear seat. At 1615, the two planes roared off from Tobera Airfield with Shimbo in the lead.

Twenty-three year old Tokio Shimizu hailed from Enzan City in Yamanashi Prefecture, southwest of Tokyo. He was the fourth son in a family of five boys, all of whom served in the war. Before the war, he worked in a liquor shop. Trained as a navigator and radioman, he served with the Mie Air Group in Japan before setting out for Rabaul.[6] He belonged to the seaplane 958th and was brought over by Commander Hori to augment his unit.

Kawato circled the airfield and climbed for altitude. Rather than trailing Shimbo towards Zungen, Kawato set his course in the opposite direction. Shimizu, who knew of Kawato's reckless nature, sensed that something was wrong. He yelled to the pilot: "Kawato! Don't do anything funny!"

Back came the reply: "Shimizu! Resign yourself to the fact that we may not return safely! We're going to bomb the enemy airfield on Green Island!" hollered Kawato over his shoulder to the incredulous observer.[7] The explanation did not sit well with Shimizu, but there was nothing he could do.

Shimbo was stymied by bad weather not long after take-off. Rather than foolishly forge ahead, he aborted the mission and returned

Green Island was socked in by heavy clouds. Undaunted, Kawato and Shimizu discussed their options. They decided to turn around and proceed back to New Britain for Zungen as they had plenty of fuel, and Commander Hori would never know of their slight de-

viation. Groping their way through the thick clouds, they flew past Wide Bay where their target was located.

About ten miles southwest of Cape Orford, Kawato and Shimizu spotted an Australian motor launch (114' gunboat) through a hole in the clouds at 6,000 feet. "Shimizu, look what we have here!" yelled Kawato with eager anticipation. "Don't send any messages yet - we're going to attack!"[8]

The lone target was ML-825, a Type B Fairmile powered by two 650 horsepower petrol engines with a top speed of twenty knots and a range of 840 nautical miles. The Royal Australian Navy operated them as anti-submarine patrol craft.

Lieutenant Harold Venables, skipper of the ML-825, was cruising her along at twelve knots with a cracked exhaust manifold on one of the engines. They were proceeding toward Jacquinot Bay. Able Seaman Eric Matthews was preparing a brew of tea in the mess deck when all hell broke loose. Enemy aircraft!

Gunners manned their battle stations as the black speck dove on them. Kawato dropped one cluster bomb from about 1,500 feet, the bombs landing about thirty yards from the target. He flew on for about a mile, turned around, then straightened out for a strafing run. The gunners on ML-825 opened up with Bofors (40mm light anti-aircraft cannon). The opening burst around the Zero momentarily stunned and disoriented Kawato. Other gunners responded with their 20mm cannon and machine guns when the aircraft was a thousand yards out. Due to the partially crippled condition of his ship and the need for a stable gun platform, Venables took no evasive action, preparing to make a stand and slug it out.[9]

Kawato lined up ML-825 in his reflector gunsight and opened fire from 600 yards. He was seen to fire three short bursts. A double line of angry white spray stitched the sea in its deadly path straight toward the vessel while the gunners hammered away.

ML-825 received nine hits. One 20mm shell slammed into the ship's forecastle and the other in the petty officer's cabin. Upper deck damage by cannon fire consisted of hits to the machine gun magazine locker, engine room ventilator and the rear depth charge Y-gun. Kawato also managed to place some minor holes on the deck with machine gun fire.

**Royal Australian Navy motor launch, ML-825. (Credit: Bob Piper)**

Three of the crewmen received superficial shrapnel wounds. Ordinary Signaler W.L. Crowe, manning the rear .303, was hit in the left chest. Able Seaman K.R. Farrington behind the midship Oerlikon, received a hit on his right thigh. Able Seaman F.W. Thompson working the No.2 midship Oerlikon caught a sliver in his right biceps.

"I was standing behind the after Oerlikon and observed the bursts of fire entering the plane," reported Venables. "The signalman, Ordinary Signalman Crowe, handled the bridge point five G.O.V. gun and after being hit by shrapnel, carried on firing until the plane had passed over."[10]

With all guns bearing on him, Kawato never had a chance. Although he had achieved an element of surprise on his unsuccessful dive bombing run, the gunners had now found their mark. Rather than veering away, the Zero continued its straight line course. Brave or foolish, Kawato didn't waiver.

Bright red projectiles drifted lazily up toward the Zero, then hit with a vengeance. Kawato was slammed back into his seat; the right wing fuel tank exploded. Bullets ripped through the thin fuselage and Shimizu slumped forward, mortally wounded. Kawato's only thought now was to escape. A fireball roared over ML-825 as the gunners gave it some parting shots.

The flaming Zero flew on for about a mile, gradually descending toward the sea. Kawato jettisoned the other bomb just before touching down. The Zero skipped across the water, then nosed in. Kawato was slammed violently forward, but his harness held and he quickly unbuckled himself and scrambled over the side. Tokio Shimizu, who was either dead or badly wounded in the rear seat, went down with the plane.

ML-825 proceeded to the crash site. When it was about a half mile distant, the plane's wing tip appeared momentarily, then sank. The crew made a thorough search of the area, but nothing was found.[11]

The entire attack had lasted only forty-two seconds. Total number of rounds fired were as follows: eighteen Bofors, forty-two Oerlikon 20mm, and fifty rounds of .303 plus an unknown quantity of .50s. The gun crew, whose average age was under twenty, performed admirably under fire. All gunners placed hits on the Zero.[12]

"I wonder if Kawato ever realized that we had added a pair of .50 caliber heavy machine guns to our own AA weapons?" writes Hal Venables. "They cost me a bottle of Scotch each and were serviced and re-armed for a cost of two bottles of beer on our return from patrols!" He further adds: "Yes, I would willingly share a good bottle with my old adversary if we ever meet. I discovered long ago that hatred is a destructive folly and I hold no animosity to any of our one time enemies."[13]

Lt. Harold Venables, RAN, commanding ML-825 (Credit: Bob Piper)

Harold Venables went into lamb raising after his discharge, but after ten years, the sea called him back. He spent the next nineteen years building yachts. He is now retired and resides in Bermagui, Australia. ML-825 was sold as war surplus on 24 January 1948 and its present whereabouts, if it still exists, is unknown.

Petty Officer First Class Kawato successfully eluded the Aussies by keeping his head down. He reached shore near East Owen Point after swimming more than a mile and a half, waterlogged and exhausted. His near-fatal encounter with ML-825 left him with a slight concussion and a broken wrist.[14]

Kawato was captured five days after his attack on ML-825, on 14 March 1945 at Baien, a few miles inland from Cape Orford. The desperate pilot had wandered aimlessly in the jungle, trying to follow the coastline. He had received no survival training and had not eaten in five days. Luckily for him, he was spotted by a native, who quickly brought others. They marched their prisoner to their camp where he was fed.

Natives from the Australian New Guinea Administrative Unit (ANGAU) delivered Kawato to the Australian 6th Infantry Brigade at Jacquinot Bay, which in turn, passed him on to the 5th Division Provost Company.[15]

A Kate torpedo bomber of the type operated from Rabaul. (Credit: Lambert)

Kawato's capture was, for him, a blessing in disguise; he would never have survived in the hostile jungle environment.

Back at Rabaul, Yasushi Shimbo heard of Kawato's capture through an intercepted radio transmission.[16] Strangely, news of his capture was not disseminated. Shigeo Terao (now Shigeo Aso), a radioman of a torpedo bomber, recalls:

> "He said he was going to Green Island. When he didn't return, I thought he must have made an emergency landing somewhere."[17]

Kawato and Shimizu were officially declared killed in action on 9 March 1945.

1. Correspondence from Tomoyoshi Hori, 8 September 1992.
2. Interrogation of Japanese Aircrew, 4.
3. Correspondence from Yoshino Ikeda, 1992.
4. Interview with Tomoyoshi Hori, Temple City, CA, 20 October 1993.
5. Prisoner of War Preliminary Interrogation Report of Masajiro Kawato, 2.
6. Correspondence from Jiro Yoshida, 9 September 1992.
7. *Zero-Sen Rabaul Ni Ari.*
8. Ibid.
9. Action Report of ML-825 by commanding officer, 10 March 1945, Royal Australian Navy, file No. 2026-27-14.
10. Ibid. "G.O.V gun" referred to by Venables means "Gas Operated Vickers." This was the standard medium gun of the British and Commonwealth Armies in both .303 and .50 calibers. It was water-cooled and belt-fed, and enjoyed the reputation of being absolutely reliable.
11. Ibid.
12. Report of action against enemy aircraft, from commanding officer, H.M.A.M.L. 825, 10 March 1945, Ref. No. S1/B20.
13. Correspondence from Hal Venables, 25 February 1992.
14. Australian Military Forces, Report on Prisoners of War, Masajiro Kawato, Australian Archives, File PWJA161003.
15. Correspondence from Australian War Memorial, 21 May1982, ref. 449/9/113.
16. Correspondence from Yasushi (Shimbo) Kanai, 1992. It was a common Japanese tradition, especially during and after the war, for a man to adopt his wife's surname. This was done in cases where her family no longer had sons to carry on the family name.
17. Correspondence from Shigeo (Terao) Aso, 10 August 1992

# 19

# THE INTERROGATION OF MASAJIRO KAWATO

Masajiro Kawato was marched into Jacquinot Bay on 17 March 1945. The five foot five 120 pound prisoner was well treated and adequately fed. He was issued a prisoner of war identification number JA-161003. Although he initially believed that Allied Forces would execute him, those fears were soon gone. There were no thoughts of escape; for him, the war was over.

Kawato was "dead" as far as his companions and family were concerned. His failure to evade capture at any cost (including suicide) was considered the ultimate disgrace. Having accepted his predicament, Kawato decided to cooperate. After all, who would ever know?

On 24 March 1945, the preliminary interrogation of Kawato began. Major R. E. M. Cameron of the Allied Translation and Interrogation Section (ATIS) interrogated the prisoner. Although it was noted that Kawato spoke some English, the session was conducted in Japanese. Kawato told Major Cameron the details of his last flight, including the strafing attack on an Allied PT boat. Next came his personal chronology, which included assignments to flight training at various air bases utilizing the Type 96 and Zero fighters, then his arrival at Rabaul.[1]

According to the report, Kawato stated that he was downed four times: 11 November 1943 ("Shot down over Simpson Harbor. Parachuted to sea and swam ashore"); 15 December 1943 ("Collided in mid-air with P-39. Parachuted to sea and swam ashore"); 6 February 1944 ("Shot down over Simpson Harbour. Parachuted to sea and swam ashore"); 9 March 1945 ("Last mission. Shot down off Cape Orford.")[2]

Major Cameron skillfully played up to Kawato's pride and elicited detailed knowledge of military significance:

"Naval airfield construction personnel at Tobera Airfield are instructed to keep the airfield serviceable as long as any airplanes exist there. There are no offensive air or ground plans by SAITO Force, however, a certain area is allotted for this unit to defend. Occasional night maneuvers are being carried out to familiarize men with the chain of trenches in the TOBERA area. These trenches are about four to five feet in width and depth."

The 105th Naval Base Air Unit was described by Kawato as a force now preoccupied with gardening. Its strength was estimated to be 2,500. He estimated that the airfield construction unit, led by Lieutenant Com-

**Flight Seaman 3/C, Masajiro Kawato at Rabaul in late 1943. (Credit: Y. Izawa)**

mander Inari, had a strength of 200 men, and that his equipment consisted of three tractors, three rollers, ten trucks and six staff cars. The men were armed with nothing more than rifles.[3]

The maintenance section was commanded by Lieutenant Torakichi Nakao. Their men were armed with rifles and were a thousand strong.

Various other units consisted of the repair section (approximately twenty men); meteorological section (approximately ten men); technical, communication, guard, and administrative sections (strengths unknown).

Aircraft were said to use 91 Octane aviation fuel, which was limited. Kawato stated that they were stored in caves approximately three miles southeast of the runway. He also observed many small fuel dumps scattered about in the rain forest one mile from the south end of the runway. Motorized transports used aviation gas mixed with light oil. Ammunition supplies (anti-aircraft) were extremely low. Their fire were held to extreme minimum. Ammo dumps was said to be in unidentified caves.

Regarding the bivouac area Kawato had this to say:

"All personnel are quartered in caves approximately three miles from airstrip in direction of Kokopo, thence about 1,000 meters to right across coconut plantation to a steep sided ravine. Each cave is approximately six by six feet and fifty feet deep and fifty men are quartered in each. Each side of ravine is lined with such caves. Force HQ is also here. Prisoner was unable to pinpoint on map."

When asked to list the key officers at Rabaul, the following list of personalities were noted: Vice Admiral Kusaka (CO, Eleventh Air Wing); Rear Admiral Saito (CO, Saito Force); Rear Admiral Okumura (CO, Naval Construction Force); Commander Ikari (CO, Vunakanau Airfield); Lieutenant Commander Inari (CO, Airfield Construction Unit); Lieutenant Torakichi Nakao (CO, ground units); Ensign Chuhei Okubo (ground officer).[4]

Regarding pilot replacement he said:

"Since 10 August 1943, approximately fifty pilots with Zekes had arrived at Tobera, but they returned to Japan as their planes became unserviceable or were lost. Some went back as early as two weeks after their arrival. PW was due for rotation, but was in hospital with wounded leg when rotation took place and transportation has not since been available. Among the original forty-five pilots who came with PW, he and another were the only ones left."

The youthful pilot tried to impress Major Cameron with his prowess in aerial combat. The interrogation report noted:

"He claims eighteen kills in 200 hours combat flying, including a B-24. P-38s are easy to out-maneuver at low altitude, but difficult beyond 5,000 meters. Most of his kills were Sikorskys (Note - PW probably confused with Corsairs) from Green Island. On 15 Dec 43 collided in mid air with P-39 from Torokina or Mono Island over Cape St. George. Both pilots rescued."[5]

Major Cameron's overall assessment of Masajiro Kawato was:

"Nineteen years of age, eight years public education, three years military service. Intelligent, normally observant and answered all questions freely. He was arrogant and proud to be a pilot. Fellow prisoners in hospital consider him mentally unstable."

Was Kawato telling the truth or misleading his captors? According to Cameron: "...information obtained is considered reliable as parts that could be checked are consistent with known facts." Postwar research has verified almost all of Kawato's statement.[6]

Former Commander Tomoyoshi Hori learned of his subordinate's indiscretion in 1992. He comments: "I have a high opinion of Kawato. I think his statements in the interrogation were generally proper and right." Hori attributes Kawato's traitorous conduct to his extreme youth and inexperience. He has been more forgiving than others and adds: "I think he need not think it a disgrace because he fulfilled his last mission admirably."[7]

On 2 April 1945, Kawato was interned in Australia at the Gaythorne Prisoner of War Camp in Queensland, and on 6 August 1945, he was transferred to the custody of the US Army (Provost Marshal Dept.) for further interrogation. Kawato "returned from the dead" to his family after the war, in November 1945.

On 9 September 1992, Shiro Shimizu, 83, the eldest brother of Kawato's back seat observer (Tokio Shimizu), received an unexpected package from aviation writer/historian Henry Sakaida in California. It contained maps, the combat report of ML-825, and various other documents detailing the last fighting moments of his younger brother.

"Due to the chaos of the war, we were not notified of Tokio's death until eight months had passed," responded Shiro Shimizu. "The Ministry of Welfare simply stated that he was missing in action and presumed killed in the Solomons on March 9, 1945. There were no further details. On March 9, 1946, exactly one year after his death, we held a funeral service for him. His name and date of death were inscribed on the tombstone of our ancestral grave."[8]

The patriarch of the Shimizu Family burst into tears as the contents of the package were explained to him. Petty Officer Tokio Shimizu went on a mission and never returned. Now they knew. Tokio Shimizu had died a hero's death forty-seven years earlier.

1. **Preliminary P.O.W. Interrogation Report of Masajiro Kawato.**
2. Ibid. In Japanese Naval Aces and Fighter Units, Kawato "engaged in three ramming attacks, was hit and shot down twice, and had to parachute to safety on four other occasions." Compare this with his interrogation statement that he was shot down three times, collided once, and parachuted three times.
3. Ibid. Kawato's estimate of his unit's strength was close. The 105 Naval Base Air Unit had 2,000 members (not including the two construction units attached to it). Kawato mentioned a Lieutenant Commander Inari as CO of an airfield construction unit. Actually, he was Lieutenant Commander Goro Enari of the 28th (civilian) Construction Unit. The 28th performed functions similar to our Seabees. However, it utilized Japanese convict labor. Highly regarded by his men for his dynamic personality, Enari and his unit were highly praised for outstanding performance in the face of incredible hardships.
4. Rear Admiral Shigeo Okumura was CO of the 8th Naval Equipment Unit. Captain Soji Ikari was CO of the 105 Naval Base Air Unit at Tobera Airfield.
5. In personal conversations with former 253 Air Group veterans Sadamu Komachi and Takeo Tanimizu, they dispute Kawato's claim of 18 victories as fabrication. The Japanese referred to F4U Corsairs as "Sikorskys." Kawato claimed that most of his victories were F4Us from Green Island. Green Island was captured on 15 February 1944. F4Us did not fly missions from there until 13 March 1944, one day after Kawato's last dogfight with F4Us over Tobera Airfield! He was only in combat for three months. From 1 December 1943 until he was shot down on 6 February 1944, he flew 35 missions; some were patrol missions with no combat. Postwar research could only confirm 1.25 victories. They include a collision with a RNZAF P-40 on 17 December 1943 and one Marine PBJ on the night of 22 March 1944 with three other pilots.
6. Most of the confirmation comes from the *United States Strategic Bombing Survey*, statements from several former Rabaul veterans, Tomoyoshi Hori (executive officer of Kawato's unit), and Allied military records.
7. Correspondence from Tomoyoshi Hori, 12 January 1992.
8. Correspondence from Shiro Shimizu, 17 November 1992.

# 20

# DARING NIGHT ATTACK

By April 1945, Allied Forces in the Admiralties were lulled into believing that Rabaul had been beaten down and no longer posed a threat. The 9 November 1944 raid on Momote Airstrip should have convinced them that the Japanese were capable of anything. The great Allied base was about to be burned again.

On 22 April, a two-seat Zero piloted by Yasushi Shimbo and carrying Ensign Chuhei Okubo, made a reconnaissance flight to the Admiralties. At 1400 hours, flying at 21,000 feet, they were astonished to discover enemy warships serenely anchored in Seeadler Harbor: two small aircraft carriers, two battleships or large cruisers, three cruisers, five destroyers, and ten transports.[1] When they returned with the news, all attention was focused on the two carriers.

Admiral Kusaka wanted those carriers! A formal directive came down from the headquarters of the Southeastern Fleet to the 105th Naval Base Air Unit: "Between April 25th and the 31st, two attack planes will attack enemy warships at berth in the Admiralty Islands in a decisive action."[2]

Plans were quickly drawn up to make a torpedo plane attack the following day. However, one of the torpedo planes was out of commission and undergoing repairs, so the attack was postponed. It was then decided to strike on the moonlit eve of the 27th.

That day Shimbo and Okubo again set off in their Zero reconnaissance plane to reconfirm the presence of the two carriers. Incredibly, the flat tops were

Ens. Chuhei Okubo, a veteran of the Pearl Harbor raid. (Credit: Y. Ikeda)

still there but heavy cloud cover ruined attack plans until the next night.

During the daylight hours of the 28th, Chief Petty Officer Gensaku Aoki and Petty Officer Isao Kochi (observer) went snooping back to the Admiralties in the two-

Under extremely formal circumstances an unidentified pilot receives orders to scout the Admiralties in the two-seat recon Zero. (Credit: Maru)

What Zero pilots from Rabaul might have seen on a reconnaissance of Seeadler Harbor, the Admiralties. The two large vessels in the background, seen through haze, could be mistaken for aircraft carriers but are actually floating dry docks. (Credit: D.J. Duxbury)

seat Zero. Their luck held; the primary targets were still there. It was almost too good to be true. Their observations were very reassuring to Admiral Kusaka and his staff. By this time, the second torpedo plane was now fully repaired and ready for action.

The ambitious plan called for two aircraft to navigate over 300 nautical miles of open sea at night, undetected by enemy radar and nightfighters, through potentially bad weather, strike their targets, and return safely to base. The crews had no experience working together under combat conditions. Their actual flight training in the Kates amounted to a mere twenty hours. They had made only three practice torpedo drops.[3]

Rear Admiral Eisho Saito and Commander Tomoyoshi Hori briefed the torpedo plane crews. Their audacious surprise attack, delivered in the dead of night, was a shot in the dark. Commander Hori recalls: "We didn't give the crews any special instructions because we didn't think the enemy would be able to guess our plans. This attack was never a suicide mission and there was no necessity for it at the time."[4] Admiral Kusaka admonished them to do their best - the integrity of the Imperial Navy rested on their shoulders.

The lead torpedo plane was to be piloted by twenty-nine year-old Ensign Tokuya Takahashi. The native from Aomori Prefecture in Northern Honshu had entered the Navy in 1936 and was an accomplished pilot. He had arrived at Rabaul in early 1942 and had survived a mid-air collision and crash landing in January 1944. As a result of this accident, he limped badly. Ensign Chuhei Okubo, who was a navigator, sat behind Takahashi and acted as the mission leader. Chief Petty Officer Shigeo Terao (radioman) rounded out the three-man crew.

Aircraft No.2 was piloted by Chief Petty Officer Jiro Nagai, a twenty-two year-old from Tokushima Prefecture in Southern Japan. He had become grounded in early 1944 when his aircraft's undercarriage broke upon landing at Vunakanau. When his unit retired to Truk, he remained behind. Nagai's team consisted of Petty Officer First Class Yoshio Sakamoto (observer) and Petty Officer Second Class Nobuo Miwata (radioman).

The six crewmen saluted their commanders and bolted to their planes. Ensign Okubo yelled a last bit of advice to the pilot of aircraft No.2: "Nagai, stick tightly

A Kate torpedo bomber from Rabaul being surrendered at Jacquinot Bay. This particular aircraft was flown by Ens. Tokuya Takahashi during the April attack on the anchorage in the Admiralties. (Credit: D. J. Duxbury)

An overhead view of Seeadler Harbor, Admiralty Islands, shows dry docks No. 4 (left) and No. 2. From 21,000 feet it is understandable that the two vessels might have looked like aircraft carriers to Japanese scouts. (Credit: USN)

to us! If we can avoid the enemy on our flight, we can succeed!" Back came the reply: "I understand! I'll be right there!"[5]

At 2010, the two Kates roared off into the moonlit sky from Vunakanau. Hundreds of personnel, including Admiral Kusaka, lined the airstrip and waved them off. In a few minutes, they were passing over Cape Lambert on the northwestern tip of New Britain Island.

The pair of aircraft climbed to 6,000 feet and maintained this altitude for the first half of the flight to the Admiralties. Jiro Nagai clung to the left rear of the lead aircraft and never left his position. Then they dropped down between 300 and 600 feet and droned on and on over a featureless expanse of ocean.

Poor weather conditions presented a major obstacle for the raiders. The forecast for the route was unreliable. Their base tried to transmit weather data, but it was not received.

Admiral Kusaka was apprehensive and waited patiently for their coded wireless communication. There was only one attempt to contact the base; the raiders worried that enemy radar operators would discover their approach through their transmissions.[6]

A large shape appeared over the horizon. Rambutyo Island! They were right on course and only forty miles from their target. The pair of Kates dropped their altitude to 150 feet; it was a smart move. The LW/AW radar, operated by the Australians, was located near sea level. Its effective range for aircraft flying at such low altitude was less than twenty miles.[7]

It was now fifteen minutes to the point of attack. Radio operator Shigeo Terao sweated out the approach.

Their position, enemy radar, and aircraft No.2 were on his mind. "Our plan was to maintain our formation and attack one carrier together," he remembers.[8]

An omen of good fortune appeared. About ten miles out, they spotted a searchlight beacon at Momote Strip, pointing straight up and flashing! It was good evidence that they had not been detected. The bad weather began to clear as they made landfall.[9] The view was breathtaking.

"The whole place was lit up, including the flare path at Momote and we could have easily landed there," said Okubo. It reminded him of prewar Tokyo's garish Ginza district at night. The area was carpeted with lights that twinkled like diamonds from the air. "There were about thirty ships in the harbor, all fully lighted and we had no difficulty identifying the target which was in the same place as it had been sighted two days earlier."[10]

Ensign Takahashi's mind was working feverishly as he would only get one chance. This is where teamwork came in. As the pilot, he was responsible for setting up the target. The navigator's job was to check the altimeter and release the torpedo upon command. The rear gunner kept their tail clear and watched for results.

As they flew over the jutting peninsula of Los Negros, Terao was overwhelmed at the large assembly of cargo ships in the harbor. But where was their target? "We made a right turn and there it was!" remembers the former radioman.[11]

"There's the carrier!" yelled Okubo excitedly to the pilot. Takahashi was one step ahead of him already banking forty degrees and leveling out for the final run against a large silhouette sitting right in the middle of the harbor. They had achieved the element of surprise.

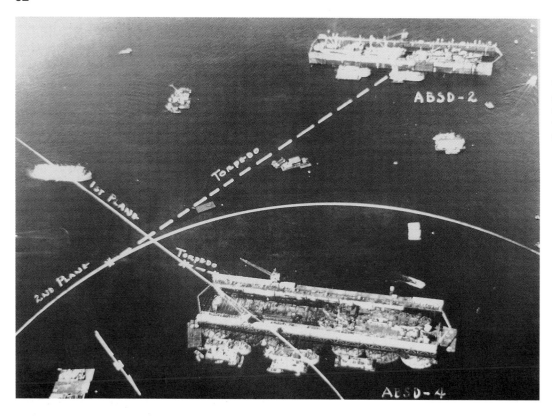

The path of the Japanese attackers on the Seeadler dry docks is portrayed on this overhead photo. (Credit: USN)

Terao jumped into action and repeatedly tapped out the telegraphic one letter code to Rabaul which meant: "We are commencing our attack!" Then the radioman slid back the canopy and brought out his 7.7mm swivel gun to defend against enemy nightfighters.[12]

The confusing array of lighted ships in the harbor and the abrupt turn may have confused Nagai, piloting No.2. The two Kates became separated at this point and it is believed that the pilot of No. 2 decided to attack another target.

Twenty-five year old Chief Carpenter Brantner Sraver was dressing in his quarters on a barge, a floating shipfitter. The ship repair technician thought he heard a plane coming in and believed it was the midnight mail plane. Then he heard more planes. Wondering what was happening, he stepped outside on the deck to investigate. His curiosity would nearly kill him.

The Japanese commenced their attack at 2315 with Chief Petty Officer Jiro Nagai delivering the first blow. He was flying twenty to twenty-five feet off the water, slowly and deliberately. Two hundred yards from his target, he dropped his 1,800 pound tin fish. Seconds later, it detonated with a thunderous blast.

For Ensign Takahashi, in the other Kate, this was his finest moment. "Range, 1,000 meters!" he shouted. The monstrous flattop grew in size as they closed the distance. He couldn't miss – it was a sitting duck. It was going to be so easy. With cool calculation, Takahashi called out "Ready!" as he steadied his plane. A few seconds later over the droning noise of the engine, the pilot signaled the release: "Pull!"

Okubo: "I pulled the lever with all of my might. The heavy torpedo detached from the aircraft and we suddenly floated upward."[13] The aircraft shot forward at a tremendous clip and passed over the ship's deck.

Chief Carpenter Sraver saw the explosion in the distance.

"I yelled for my men to turn off the lights. I ran over on the dry dock to get the power turned off. I was headed to the quarter deck which was on the opposite side of the dry dock and I knew the officer of the deck could not see what was taking place. There was a catwalk that went between the wingwalk and that is where I met the duty electrician. I told him we were under attack and to go back and kill the lights...just as I came out from between the wingwalk, I first saw the plane and it was headed straight towards me. I saw a splash in the water and the plane went right over my head."[14]

Takahashi's Kate roared over the deck of the ship by a few feet, and Ensign Okubo could see the stunned faces of a couple of workmen. About five or six seconds after clearing the target, Takahashi banked his plane to the right and climbed for altitude.

"Terao, any hits yet?" yelled Okubo over his shoulder. "No, not yet!" came the reply. The waiting was horrendous.

Takahashi's torpedo ran true; it slid under Sraver's barge and slammed into the target. The terrific explosion blew Sraver right off the dock and into the water. He came up under the dry dock and banged his head; he was pulled out of the water by two men. Thirty-seven men on the barge received minor injuries, mostly from flying glass.

Okubo and Terao saw a huge column of white water shoot high into the sky like a slow motion movie. "We hit it, we hit it, we hit it!" screamed Terao in wild jubilation.

Ensign Takahashi completed his turn and reached the entrance to the harbor, but aircraft No.2 was nowhere in sight. So sudden was their attack that no anti-aircraft guns responded. When No. 2 didn't show up at the rendezvous point after waiting a few minutes, Takahashi headed out to sea. In a few minutes, they were over Rambutyo Island.

Terao brought out his hand signaling device and flashed out messages into the dark. He knew that enemy nightfighters might be lurking in the area, but they had to do something.[15] Where could No.2 be?

Takahashi directed his aircraft toward Kavieng on the northern tip of New Ireland. When the pilot sighted New Hanover Island, he checked his fuel gauge; there was enough fuel for another two hours of flight. Rabaul was 180 miles away - another hour and a half. Takahashi conferred with Okubo about the dilemma, but both were unfamiliar with Kavieng Airfield and the thought of a night landing there was disturbing. It was decided to continue toward Rabaul.[16]

Around 0200, Takahashi spotted the distinctive cone of the 640 foot Mt. Hanabuki (Tavurvur), one of Rabaul's two active volcanoes. Relief, joy, and weariness filled their hearts. In a few minutes, they glided

**Brantner Sraver (Credit: Sraver)**

**Torpedo damage to one of the pontoons of Dry Dock No. 2 is fully disclosed after the dock is raised. Only the integrity of this single pontoon was compromised by the damage. (Credit: USN)**

ABSD 2 - Damage to pontoon disclosed after raising dock.

A close-up view of Dry Dock No. 4 shows one large merchant ship and smaller auxiliaries awaiting repair. From masthead level, in the dark, it is possible to understand how the Japanese attackers thought they were approaching a sizable warship. (Credit: USN)

into Vunakanau Airfield and were met by Lieutenant Torakichi Nakao, chief of the airfield ground unit and some guards. They climbed into a truck and slowly made their way to headquarters.

Ensign Okubo immediately informed the senior officers of the plight of No.2 and asked that searchlights be turned on. Commander Hori relayed the urgent request to headquarters. Anti-aircraft searchlights on top of the hill surrounding the airfield briefly lit up the sky like a Hollywood premiere. If Nagai was lost, the searchlights would be his savior. With each passing minute, hope faded. Nagai and his faithful crew never returned. Admiral Kusaka's elation at their success was tempered by the loss of three young men and it weighed heavily on his mind.

At their debriefing, Ensign Okubo stated:

"We attacked and sank a small aircraft carrier. The Americans were caught completely off guard. They hadn't expected a night torpedo attack from Rabaul! The ships and harbor were well illuminated. As soon as our torpedo struck, all the deck lights went off. I saw the water rise in a spout and there was a large whirlpool on the sea. I last saw Nagai making a run on a battleship."[17]

The "aircraft carrier" and "battleship" that were reported sunk were actually floating docks (Advanced Base Sectional Docks)! They were not sunk, but did suffer moderate damage. Nagai's torpedo struck the ABSD-4's rear pontoon directly underneath the side wall, rupturing the hull. Takahashi's torpedo damaged a compartment on one of ABSD-2's attending pontoons.[18] From a distance the recon crews had thought that the two dry docks were aircraft carriers. During the night low level approach by the Kates the pair of dry docks indeed looked like carriers or battleships in profile.

Regarding Nagai's attack the American battle report stated: "After dropping the torpedo, the plane climbed sharply, making a steep right bank over the starboard sidewall and barely missing the crane. The pilot seemed to loose control, and the plane fell sideways into the harbor."[19]

"That torpedo had my initials on it, but luckily not my name!" said Sraver. "I could have been killed. I was injured and I do have a Purple Heart presented to me for that incident. We had no idea that anything like that could happen. After all, the war was coming to an end; at least we thought so. We were working around the clock with all lights turned on. Welding machines and burning torches going full blast. The light from them could be seen for miles."[20]

Branter Sraver retired as an officer from the Navy in 1958 and resides in Norfolk, Virginia. Now 72 years old, he is shooting for 105.

The exact circumstances surrounding the loss of Jiro Nagai's aircraft is still a mystery. In his interrogation statements to the Australians after the war, Chuhei Okubo stated that Nagai joined up on their starboard side after the attack and was with them for about thirty miles. They sailed into bad weather again and No.2 broke off to the right and was not see again. American divers failed to find any trace of the Kate where it supposedly crashed into the harbor.

"Certainly Okubo's statement and the American eyewitness reports are contradictory," remarks Terao (Aso). "This is the first time I have heard of it! I am very surprised to see the American reports and photographs concerning our attack!"[21]

Commander Hori had believed ever since the war, that they had sunk an aircraft carrier. After studying the American damage report and accompanying photographs, he remarked:

"Seeing your Navy report concerning the torpedo attack, I could admit now that the target we hit was a floating dry dock and not an aircraft carrier. Even if there was no brilliant result, we were proud of the night torpedo attack carried out under those difficult circumstances. It raised the morale of our whole force in Rabaul and struck terror into the enemy's heart!"[22]

Ensign Chuhei Okubo believed they scored one carrier for the Navy and nothing could change his mind.

"Immediately after the war, I heard words spoken by the Americans that what we hit was a floating dock. Let me respond to that. Three years before the start of the war, I served aboard aircraft carriers. I have absolute confidence in my warship identification. When we flew over that ship, there appeared to be a flight deck. That's what it looked like. It couldn't have been anything else but a carrier."[23]

1. *Rabaul Sen Sen Ijo Nashi.*
2. *Rabaul Kokutai Nao Kanto Su* (Rabaul's Naval Air Group Fought Bravely), Konnichi No Wadai Publishers, Tokyo, undated excerpt from Yoshinobu Ikeda. The author was Chuhei Okubo and it was written in the late 1950s or early 1960s.
3. Ibid.
4. Correspondence from Tomoyoshi Hori, 16 February 1992.
5. *Rabaul Kokutai Nao Kanto Su.*
6. Correspondence with Ed Simmonds, 9 December 1994. He writes: "...It is surprising to me that the Japanese insisted on aircraft transmitting messages during a mission. This was a 'give away' for the flying boat which was the first to bomb Townsville in 1942. RAAF signals followed their hourly transmissions and D/F'ed them all the way from Rabaul and so were able to forecast that Townsville was the target. They also forecast the ETA (estimated time of arrival) correctly but unfortunately no one took any notice but no damage was done."
7. Ibid. Simmonds, a former Australian radar operator who was familiar with the radar setup on Los Negros, stated that they would have had "maybe 10 minutes warning if immediately detected except for the fact that the info would have had to go through Fighter Sector, etc., but there is no evidence that they were picked up by the radar."
8. Correspondence from Shigeo (Terao) Aso, 10 August 1992.
9. Interrogation of Japanese Aircrew, 8.
10. *Rabaul Kokutai Nao Kanto Su.*
11. Aso.
12. *Rabaul Kokutai Nao Kanto Su.*
13. Ibid.
14. Correspondence from Brantner Sraver, 11 November 1992.
15. Aso.
16. *Rabaul Kokutai Nao Kanto Su.*
17. Ibid. Okubo's report was confirmed in an interview with Tomoyoshi Hori, Temple City, CA, 20 October 1993.
18. War Diary of Naval Base, Navy 3205, April 1945, Serial 00948. ABSD-2 was capable of 100,000 tons lift; ABSD-4, 70,000 tons. The floating docks were located at Lombrum Point on Los Negros Island inside Seeadler Harbor. The Manus Island bases in the Admiralty Islands were the third largest advance base in the Pacific, after Guam and Leyte (Philippines).
19. Action Report by Commander Naval Base Manus, Admiralty Islands, Serial 00952, 9 May 1945.
20. Sraver.
21. Aso.
22. Correspondence from Tomoyoshi Hori, 5 April 1992.
23. *Rabaul Kokutai Nao Kanto Su.*

**Takahashi's B5N Kate after the surrender. (Credit: B.B. Cox)**

# 21

# THE WAR'S END

The war was winding down, but Rabaul's defenders didn't know it; it was business as usual. Lack of spare parts and able-bodied pilots hampered their ability to conduct even minimal flight operations. There were no reconnaissance missions to the Admiralties after the 28 April night torpedo attack. However, local flights over and around Rabaul continued as evidenced by reports from RNZAF aircrews. The 958th Air Group's Jakes continued communication and ferry flights. Many owed their lives to these aircrews who delivered medical supplies under most dangerous conditions.

Buin Airfield HQ notified Rabaul in July that their mechanics had remanufactured a Zero from wrecks.[1] This A6M3 Model 22 had been badly damaged in November 1943. To prevent destruction, they wheeled it off the strip and hid it from view.

The officers at Buin had heard of Rabaul's 108th Aircraft Repair Shop and their ingenuity in remanufacturing operational aircraft from wrecks. But Buin also had capable mechanics and engineers, and a serviceable hulk hidden in the bushes. It was decided to rebuild this aircraft to give their idle technical staff a boost in morale. Their plan was to present Rabaul with one of their own custom-built aircraft.

In mid-July, the Zero was completed. The airframe was rebuilt from components of many damaged aircraft and sported the tail number 2-182.[2] Buin HQ radioed Rabaul and requested a pilot to test fly, then ferry the aircraft to Rabaul. Petty Officer Sekizen Shibayama was selected for this task and ferried to Buin in a Jake floatplane. He was awaiting departure orders when the surrender came.

"In August, hundreds of US boats appeared off the island and the Japanese Army was about to do a Banzai attack against them," remembers Shibayama. "I was ordered to attack them with this single Zero. Fortunately, HQ heard that the war was over on August 17th or so. Thus, the attack was called off and I survived. Some mechanics told me that I would be killed immediately after the Americans land. I felt scared but nothing happened."[3]

On 15 August 1945, the Emperor formally announced a surrender. Commander Hori remembers:

"That day, the notice by telegram came to Admiral Kusaka from Tokyo. Admiral Kusaka summoned the high ranking officers of each unit in Rabaul to headquarters. At first, he read the words of the Emperor and gave instructions to us. During his speech, his words often died on his lips and he was moved to tears, and we all were moved to tears also.[4]

"Rear Admiral Saito and I returned to the 105th Air Corps and announced the surrender to the entire unit," Hori continues. "All the members grew excited and many of them wept bitterly. That night, several members committed suicide."[5]

Imperial Headquarters in Tokyo issued an explicit directive that all fighting must cease immediately, otherwise, violation of the surrender terms would have serious consequences for Japan. Diehards, both in Japan and at Rabaul, vowed to continue fighting. Their inventory of aircraft at the time of surrender were three

The A6M3 Model 22 No. 2-182 that was remanufactured from wrecks by mechanics and engineers at Buin (Kara) Airfield. Sekizen Shibayama was assigned to fly this aircraft in the final Banzai attack against enemy shipping off Bougainville, but the war ended before the sortie could be launched. (Credit: C. Darby via Jim Lansdale)

RNZAF officers brief Japanese pilots at Rabaul about the final surrender flight to Jacquinot Bay. New Zealanders are unknown. Japanese are (L. to R.) Army Capt. Nario Iwanaga, and fighter pilots Gensaku Aoki, Yoshio Otsuki and Yasushi Shimbo, the flight leader. (RNZAF via D.J. Duxbury)

Zero fighters, one Kate torpedo plane, one Dinah twin-engined recon plane and two Jakes (twin-float reconnaissance aircraft).

"By Admiral Kusaka's order, we high ranking officers visited each unit by car in order to dissuade our men from fighting," says Hori. "At last, the whole force in Rabaul became calm and we waited for the arrival of the occupation forces. About two months later, the Australian Occupation Force came to Rabaul with exaggerated movement as if it was landing in the face of the enemy."[6]

Seven Allied prisoners of war remained in the prison stockade at Tunnel Hill. They were: Lieutenants James A. McMurria, Jose L. Holguin, and Alfonse D. Quinones; Lieutenant (j.g.) Joseph G. Nason, Sergeant Escoe Palmer, Petty Officer First Class John P. Kepchia,

and Captain John J. Murphy. It was around nine o'clock on the morning of 16 August 1945. These seven were the lucky ones out of more than seventy-five who had perished through malnutrition, disease, and medical neglect. Warrant Officer Torataro Matsumoto, commandant of the camp, arrived and took a seat at a small table and began to address his prisoners: "The war between Japan and America is finished; America has won. From this moment you are no longer prisoners of war, you are gentlemen."[7]

Even though the war had ended, there were still important tasks to be completed. Ensign Tokuya Takahashi and his crew flew a relief mission on 18 August; they dropped medical supplies to survivors on Buka Island. Vital military records were burned.

Vice Admiral Jin-Ichi Kusaka, representing the Southeast Area Fleet, and Lieutenant General Hitoshi

The last three Zeroes of Rabaul's guerrilla air force are shown with engines turning just prior to their last flight on 18 Sep 1945. The pilots were Gensaku Aoki, Yoshio Otsuki and Yasushi Shimbo. (Credit: RNZAF)

**WO Yasushi Shimbo taxis out for his final surrender flight to Jacquinot Bay. (Credit: RNZAF)**

Imamura (Eighth Area Army) surrendered Rabaul to the Australians in a ceremony that took place on the aircraft carrier HMS *Glory* on 6 September 1945. They relinquished their swords to General Vernon A.H. Sturdee, commanding the First Australian Army. There was stoical acceptance of surrender by the Japanese and their only thoughts now were of home and their families.

They were in for a rude shock. The harsh conditions that endured during the war years failed to subside once the surrender took place. The 100,000 Japanese on Rabaul were put into ten camps and members of the Kempei Tai (Army military police) were employed to keep the peace.

A former member of the 6th Field Kempei Tai, recalls the bitter memories of this period:

"Regarding the treatment by rank of Japanese forces after demobilization, their position would be that of disarmed Japanese, and they would not be accorded POW treatment, according to orders delivered by the commander. Being disarmed Japanese, rather than POWs, Japanese officers and soldiers were not supplied food, clothing or medicine at all. In spite of that, the Australian Army's demand for labor was enforced. We were treated as slaves and subjected to heavy labor on the docks, in the warehouses, and in road work. For lunch, we managed to stave off starvation by taking the sweet potatoes we had grown to supplement our rations during the war, which we steamed and

took in our mess tins. It was truly a picture of hell and nothing else."[8]

Commander Hori wasn't pleased about the lack of medical supplies for his men. "About medicines, the (Australians) didn't provide to us at all. On the contrary, they took away what little we had of Atebrin (anti-malaria medicine) from our force, and I heard that quite a few patients died before returning to Japan."[9]

Lieutenant Minoru Shinohara (now Fujita) recalls the kindness of his Australian counterpart:

"I headed a crew of forty and we unloaded ships in the harbor. It was certainly hard work, but they did not mistreat my men. In fact, this Australian officer provided me with tea and soda crackers. Those soda crackers were so delicious! The Australian soldiers were very fond of our watches and two-colored pencils, so we traded them for cigarettes. They were amazed we had Japanese-made trucks. They thought we had imported them. They couldn't believe that Japan could make good trucks."[10]

In time the surviving aircraft were also surrendered. Mechanics slaved over the engines and finally had them ready for flight. On 18 September 1945, newly promoted Warrant Officer Yasushi Shimbo led Petty Officers Gensaku Aoki and Yoshio Otsuki on a flight from Vunakanau to Jacquinot Bay. Also in their group was a single Dinah reconnaissance aircraft. They were escorted by sixteen Australian fighters.

**An Army Ki-46 II Dinah recon aircraft, piloted by Japanese Army Capt. Nario Iwanaga, prepares to take-off from Rabaul on 18 Sep 1945. (Credit: Kazuhiko Osuo)**

The siege of Rabaul ends with formal surrender ceremonies of Japanese forces for New Britain and the Solomons takes place off Rabaul aboard carrier HMS *Glory*. Gen. H. Imamura presents his sword to Lt. Gen. V.A.H. Sturdee, Australian Army. Vice Adm. Kusaka is in Navy whites at far left. (Credit: Australian War Memorial)

When the Zeroes landed, the pilots stepped out on the wings of their aircraft and saluted smartly. The curious spectators milling around the aircraft ignored them and the pilots were crestfallen. One of them burst into tears. They were frisked for weapons and treated correctly. Shimbo presented two copies of a typed receipt for the aircraft to Wing Commander P.A. Matheson, the commander of Jacquinot. He was supposed to sign one and return it to General Imamura, but Matheson kept both copies. This slight agitated the Japanese pilots. They were quickly hustled aboard a Catalina flying boat and taken back to Rabaul.

The final flight mission of the 105th Naval Base Air Unit occurred on 14 October 1945. Petty Officer Goro Kataoka flew the surviving Kate torpedo bomber to Jacquinot under the watchful eyes of four 16 Squadron RNZAF Corsairs, led by Flight Sergeant Bryan Cox. On this day, the 105th Naval Base Air Unit passed into history.

1. There has been some confusion about the existence of Buin Airfield since Allied maps of the area at the time showed no such airfield. The Japanese frequently mentioned Buin Airfield. According to a letter by Sekizen Shibayama, there actually was an airfield (Navy) at Buin, but it was not in use in 1945. He wrote that there was an airfield, known locally as Toripoil, about 5 km north of Buin. This airfield was Kara. The Buin Airfield referred to by the Japanese was actually Kara Airfield.
2. Correspondence from James F. Lansdale, 12 November 1992.
3. Correspondence from Sekizen Shibayama, 17 January 1992.
4. Correspondence from Tomoyoshi Hori, 1993.
5. Ibid.
6. Ibid.
7. Private memoir of Jose L. Holguin.
8. Private memoir of a former Kempei Tai member, name withheld, April 1993.
9. Correspondence from Tomoyoshi Hori, 1 March 1993.
10. Interview with Minoru (Shinohara) Fujita, Rosemead, CA, February, 1993

# *EPILOGUE*

The accomplishments of Rabaul's 105th Naval Base Air Unit and the 958th Air Group were militarily insignificant. Their continued operation in the face of intense enemy opposition was courageous. The audacious bombing of Momote Airstrip in November 1944 by three Zeroes and the daring night torpedo attack in April 1945 boosted morale. Both the Allied Forces and the environment served to grind them down, but they carried on. In spirit and mind, they were never defeated.

When the war ended, the men returned to Japan from Rabaul and struggled for many years to rebuild their lives and their country. Very few bothered to reminisce about those horrible years; their children were not interested in what they did during the war. School textbooks gloss over World War II. When prodded by genuine interest, these old veterans will speak. Their memories may have faded, but their sense of loss for old comrades remain strong. Veteran fighter pilots who survived Rabaul are held in high adulation.

What became of the key men from this proud unit? Some of them are still around while others have passed on. Vice Admiral Jin-Ichi Kusaka, head of Naval forces on Rabaul, died on 8 August 1972 at age eighty-four. Rear Admiral Eisho Saito, commander of the 105th Naval Base Air Unit, died on 9 March 1954.

Warrant Officer Shigeo Fukumoto, who left Rabaul in April 1944 to ferry aircraft to Truk, was killed in Fuji City, Shizuoka Prefecture, on 26 December 1945. This popular and tireless warrant officer died in a car accident driving while intoxicated. He had returned to Japan from Truk aboard a submarine after refusing orders to return to Rabaul due to the slapping incident. He served for about three months with the 302nd Air Group at Atsugi (Japan) before surrender.

Petty Officer Kentaro Miyagoshi returned to Japan in March 1945 and was assigned to home defense. He served honorably with the Yokosuka Air Group. He was electrocuted in an accident shortly after the war.

Yoshinobu Ikeda was ordered to return to Japan in March 1945 for home defense duties. Like his comrade Miyagoshi, he also ended his military service with the Yokosuka Air Group. He went back to farming, but later joined the new Japan Self Defense Air Force and learned to fly helicopters. He later became a commercial helicopter pilot and is now retired. He says: "Three times at Rabaul, bombs exploded very close to me, but I survived! I was very lucky. I always believed that I would surely die in Rabaul!"

Sekizen Shibayama completed 350 combat missions, recorded over ten victories, and is now a Tokyo businessman. His Zero was recovered at Rabaul in 1972 and brought back to Bakersfield, California where he was reunited with his old mount. It was destroyed in a suspicious museum fire in San Diego a few years later. His Zero 22 from Kara Airstrip is now on display in a museum in Auckland, New Zealand.

Fumio Wako became a Yokohama policeman after the war and tries to forget about the war years.

Gensaku Aoki finished the war with 200 flight hours at Rabaul. He came home and joined the Self Defense Force as a helicopter pilot and is now retired.

Yasushi Shimbo changed his name to Kanai and is alive and well. Immediately after the war, he entered college to study textile and fibers. He became a salesman for a silk thread manufacturing company after graduation and in 1975 became president of this company. For many years, he had kept silent about his war experiences. In 1992, he decided to contribute his recollections for the sake of history. He and Bill Hopper, pilot of the Marine PBJ he attacked over Vunakanau, exchanged friendly correspondence in 1993.

Masajiro Kawato returned to Japan from captivity; he served with the Japan Self Defense Air Force until leaving for reasons that are unclear. He then worked as an airline pilot before immigrating to the United States in 1976. In the same year, he made a solo Trans-Pacific flight from Tokyo to California in a single-engined Piper Comanche. Kawato's flight was poorly documented and was never recognized as an official world record despite his claim to the contrary.

Now known as "Mike" Kawato, he resides in Redmond, Washington. In 1978, he republished his Japanese memoir into English under the title **Flight Into Conquest** (re-titled again as **Bye Bye Blacksheep**). In the book, he claims that he was the Zero pilot who downed the Marine Corps legend, "Pappy" Boyington. Subsequent research indicates that his claim is a myth. Both Kawato and Boyington would trade barbs at air shows while each promoted their own books. The remarkably youthful Kawato makes the lecture circuit and is a familiar figure around air shows across the country.

Kate torpedo plane pilot, Ensign Tokuya Takahashi, finished the war with over 2,600 flight hours and returned to Japan; his whereabouts are unknown at this time. His radioman, Shigeo Terao, changed his name to Aso, served with the Japan Self Defense Air Force as a radar technician, then later lectured at the Defense University and is now retired.

Chuhei Okubo, one of Rabaul's heroes, was alive in the late 1970s, but is now deceased. He was a rubber boot manufacturer after the war. According to surviving comrades, he became a Communist and was ostracized by his siblings and former comrades for his extreme political views. In 1976, he made plans to accompany Masajiro Kawato on a nonstop trans-Pacific flight to the United States. Kawato's Comanche could not handle the additional weight, so Okubo was left behind.

Commander Tomoyoshi Hori, executive officer of the 105 Naval Base Air Unit, brought his men home to Japan aboard US Liberty ships on 17 May 1946. He worked for various companies as a "salaried man" until his retirement with Daiwa Bank. He is now eighty-four years old, with a very sharp mind and an excellent command of English. Mr. Hori has close ties to California; some of his grandchildren were born there and he has been a frequent visitor to the Golden State.

# VETERANS OF THE SIEGE OF RABAUL

Chuhei Okubo  (Credit:  Maru)

Dr. William H. Hopper  (Credit: W.H. Hopper)

Gensaku Aoki in 1991.  (Credit: G. Aoki)

Hal Venables, skipper of ML-825  (Credit: H. Venables)

Angelo F. Bilotta in 1992 (Credit: Bilotta)

In 1971 Sekizen Shibayama was reunited with his old Zero in Bakersfield, CA.  He was shot down into Simpson Harbor in this very aircraft on 11 Nov 1943.  It was recovered by a team led by US Navy aces, Gene Valencia, Jim French and Marshall Beebe.  (Credit: Shibayama )

# VETERANS OF THE SIEGE OF RABAUL

Masajiro "Mike" Kawato in 1992. (Credit: H. Sakaida)

Veterans of VMF-222 reunited in Van Nuys, CA in 1986. (L. to R.) Don Sapp, now Stapp; George Schaefer, Winifred Reid and Robert Wilson. (Credit: R. Wilson)

Yasushi (Shimbo) Kanai at a New Zealand air museum, standing on the Zero last assigned to comrade, Shibayama. (Credit: Y. Kanai)

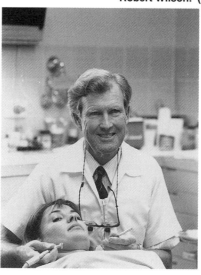

Dr. Hugh D. Kennare, early 1985. (Credit: H. Kennare)

Yoshinobu Ikeda in 1993. (Credit: Y. Ikeda)

Lt. Gen. Robert P. Keller (Ret.), on the right with former WO Sadamu Komachi at NAS Pensacola on 7 May 1992. Both fought over Rabaul. (Credit: H. Sakaida)

Comdr. Tomoyoshi Hori and author Henry Sakaida. (Credit: Sakaida)

# RABAUL'S MILITARY PRISONERS

Anderson, F.  F/O  (Australian)
RAAF
Executed, date unknown.

Arbuckle, John  Lt.  (American)
USN VP-52
Survived.

Atkiss, Daniel Davis  Ens.  (American)
USN VT-305
Died of malaria 7-29-45 in Kempei Tai prison.

Bailey, John P.  WO  (Australian)
RAAF
Executed 1944.

Barnett, Leslie  Sgt.  (American)
USAAF 33BS, 90 BG
Transported to Japan  11-43, survived.

Barron, John M.  T/Sgt.  (American)
USAAF 501BS, 345BG
Executed 3-5-44 by 6th Field Kempei Tai at Talili.

Bartoff, -  1/Lt.  (American)
USMC
Fate unknown.

Beck, Phillip  1/Lt.  (American)
USAAF 65BS, 43BG
Executed, probably in early 1944, remains recovered.

Bedkover, Douglas  1/Lt.  (Australian)
RAA
Army coastwatcher, died 1-3-44 of malaria and starvation in
Kempei Tai prison.

Berry, Alexander R.  Lt.  (American)
USN VMSB-143
Executed 3-5-44 by 6th Field Kempei Tai at Talili.

Borders Jr., Andrew J.  2/Lt.  (American)
USAAF 70 FS, 18 FG
P-39 pilot. Executed 3-5-44 by 6th Field Kempei Tai at Talili.

Boyington, Gregory  Maj.  (American)
USMC VMF-214
Transported to Japan 2-44, survived.

Boyle, Donald W.  Maj.  (American)
USMV VMF-212
Transported to Japan 2-44, survived.

Brendon, -  1/Lt.  (American)
USMC
Aviator, fate unknown.

Brindos, Roger Hugh  1/Lt.  (American)
USMC VMF-321
Executed 3-5-44 by 6th Field Kempei Tai at Talili.

Bromley, -  (Australian)
RAAF
Executed 1942.

Brown, D.S.  Sgt.  (Australian)
RAAF
Executed, date unknown.

Burnette, Leslie  T/Sgt.  (American)
USAAF  90BG
Last seen alive 11-13-43, fate unknown.

Burns, J.J.  LAC  (Australian)
RAAF
Executed, date unknown.

Callaghan, -  (American)
USAAF
Last seen alive 11-43 in Navy custody, fate unknown.

Cassera, Michael H.  (American)
USAAF
Executed 3-5-44 by 6th Field Kempei Tai at Talili.

Cassidy, Robert  Pvt.  (Australian)
RAA Aux. and Intelligence Corps
Transported to Japan 11-43, fate unknown.

Cheli, Ralph  Maj.  (American)
USAAF 38BG
Executed 3-5-44 by 6th Field Kempei Tai at Talili.

Chikowsky, -  (American)
USAAF
Executed 10-42.

Clay, Ernest Herbert  Sgt.  (Australian)
RAAF 11 Recon Sq.
Executed 3-5-44 by 6th Field Kempei Tai at Talili.

Clements, -  (American)
USAAF
According to Maj. Saiji Matsuda of 6th Field Kempei Tai, Clements
was transported to Japan and arrived safely; fate unknown.

Constantine, Edward D.  Sgt.  (American)
USAAF 72BS, 5BG
Executed 3-5-44 by 6th Field Kempei Tai at Talili.

Cornelius, Hugh Royal  2/Lt.  (American)
USMC VMTB-233
Died 4-29-44 of malaria in Kempei Tai prison.

Cox Jr., Wilston M.  Maj.  (American)
USAAF 38BG
Transported to Japan 11-43, fate unknown.

Cox, John Preson  2/Lt.  (American)
USAAF 44FS, 18FG
Executed 3-5-44 by 6th Field Kempei Tai at Talili.

Crawford, -  1/Lt.  (American)
USMC
Aviator, last seen alive 11-43 in Navy custody, fate unknown.

Crocker, -  (American)
Aviator, captured Ballale, Bougainville. Last seen alive 1-44 in
Navy custody, fate unknown.

Dale, Arthur L. Lt. (American)
USN VT-12
Fate unknown.

Dawkins, Harry B. F/Lt. (Australian)
RAAF 22 Bomb Sq.
Died in captivity 7-15-44 from beriberi and dysentery.

Diercks, F.A.D. F/O (Australian)
RAAF
Executed, date unknown.

Doyle, Thomas F. 1/Lt. (American)
USAAF 321BS, 90BG
Executed 3-5-44 by 6th Field Kempei Tai at Talili.

Engel, Fred S. Sgt. (American)
USAAF 90BG
Transported to Japan 11-43, survived.

Esband, Colin F/Lt. (Australian)
RAAF 33 Sq.
Executed 3-5-44 by 6th Field Kempei Tai at Talili.

Evans, Herschel Daniel 2/Lt. (American)
USAAF, 500BS
Executed 3-5-44 by 6th Field Kempei Tai at Talili.

Farnell, Raymond J. Sgt. (American)
USAAF 321BS, 90BG
Executed 3-5-44 by 6th Field Kempei Tai at Talili.

Fenwick, John "Jack" Sgt. (Australian)
RAAF 11Sq.
Executed 3-5-44 by 6th Field Kempei Tai at Talili.

Fessenger, Thomas Bruce 1/Lt. (American)
USAAF 5BG
Died 7-22-44 of dyspepsia (impared digestion) in Kempei Tai prison.

Fitzgerald, John Joseph 2/Lt. (American)
USMC VMF-215
Died 8-8-44 of pneumonia in Kempei Tai prison.

Gillis, John Sgt. (American)
USAAF 5BG
Died 7-28-44 of dyspepsia in Kempei Tai prison.

Gordon, Thomas Sgt. (Australian)
RAAF
Died in captivity.

Griffin, Jack Pvt. (American)
USAAF 43BG
Transported to Japan 11-43, survived.

Hanks, Bill Donald 2/Lt. (American)
USAAF 70FS, 18FG
Died 8-14-44 of beriberi in Kempei Tai prison.

Hardwick, V.H. LAC (Australian)
RAAF
Executed, date unknown.

Harris, William C. S/Sgt. (American)
USAAF 501BS, 345BG
Executed 3-5-44 by 6th Field Kempei Tai at Talili.

Heichel, Byron Capt. (American)
USAAF 63BS, 48 BG
Captured New Ireland, transported to Japan, believed survived.

Hill, Joseph W. Lt. (American)
USAAF 44FS, 18FG
Executed 3-5-44 by 6th Field Kempei Tai at Talili.

Hocking, A.R. Corp. (Australian)
RAAF
Executed, date unknown.

Holguin, Jose L. 2/Lt. (American)
USAAF 65BS, 43BG
Survived and died 3-22-94.

Huey, Wellman H. 2/Lt. (American)
USAAF 339FS, 347 FG
Captured Bougainville 2-14-43, transported to Rabaul, executed, date unknown.

Keefe, Frank George F/Lt. (New Zealander)
RNZAF 14 Sq.
Shot down and captured 1-15-45, died 1-30-45 of medical neglect.

Keel, Henry A. 2/Lt. (American)
USAAF 13BS, 3BG
Executed, date unknown.

Kelly, Cephas Pfc. (American)
USN VMSB-143
Transported to Japan 11-43, survived.

Kepchia, John Pozer PO1/c (American)
USN VT-305
Survived.

Kicera, Michael H. Sgt. (American)
USAAF 501BS, 345BG
Executed 3-5-44 by 6th Field Kempei Tai at Talili.

King, A.C. (American)
USAAF
Executed 10-42.

Kirkwood, Donald Francis F/Sgt. (Australian)
RAAF 30 Sq.
Executed 3-5-44 by 6th Field Kempei Tai at Talili.

Koebig, Fredrick I. Maj. (American)
USAAF 5BG
Executed 3-5-44 by 6th Field Kempei Tai at Talili.

Kraehe, Ernest H. (Australian)
RAAF
Executed 3-5-44 by 6th Field Kempei Tai at Talili.

Krishner, Kenneth Donald 1/Lt. (American)
USAAF 5FS
Executed 3-5-44 by 6th Field Kempei Tai at Talili.

Kuhn, Anthony 2/Lt. (American)
USAAF 394BS
Executed 3-5-44 by 6th Field Kempei Tai at Talili.

Lanagan, A.H. Corp. (Australian)
RAAF
Executed, date unknown.

Lanigan, Richard R. CPO (American)
USN VT-305
Died 7-30-45 of dyspepsia in Kempei Tai prison.

Lanphier, Charles Cox  2/Lt.  (American)
USMC VMF-214
Brother of Capt. Tom Lanphier Jr. (Yamamoto Mission). Died 5-15-44 of beriberi in Kempei Tai prison.

Mannon, Paul M.  (American)
USN
Executed, probably in 1944.

Marr, Romulus F.  (American)
USAAF
Executed 3-5-44 by 6th Field Kempei Tai at Talili.

Martindale, Robert L.  1/Lt.  (American)
USAAF  33BS, 90BG
Transported to Japan, survived.

Mason, C.J.T.  F/O  (Australian)
RAAF
Executed by 81st Guards Unit 9-42.

Massey, -  (American)
USAAF
Executed 10-42.

Mayberry, Walter Thomas  1/Lt.  (American)
USMC VMF-123
Captured in the Solomons 9-2-43, executed 3-5-44 by 6th Field Kempei Tai at Talili.

McCauley, Paul F.  (American)
USAAF
Executed 3-5-44 by 6th Field Kempei Tai at Talili.

McCleaf, Paul Fredrick  Corp.  (American)
USMC VMSB-341
Executed 3-5-44 by 6th Field Kempei Tai at Talili.

McCown, Marion R.  Capt.  (American)
USMC VMF-321
Shot down 1-15-44 and captured, fate unknown.

McDonald, E.J.  LAC  (Australian)
RAAF
Executed, date unknown.

McFarlane, John O.  F/Lt.  (New Zealander)
RNZAF 16 Sq.
May have been transported to Japan, fate unknown.

McLellan-Symonds, Leslie  F/O  (New Zealander)
RNZAF  25 Sq.
Died 5-25-44 of malaria and untreated bullet wound in thigh.

McMurria, James Austin  2/Lt.  (American)
USAAF 321BS, 90BG
Survived.

Miller, James L.  Lt(jg)  (American)
USN VF-17
Died 5-7-45 of beriberi.

Mull, Romulus F.  Sgt.  (American)
USAAF 313BG
Executed 3-5-44 by 6th Field Kempei Tai at Talili.

Murphy, Henry Lawrence  F/Sgt.  (Australian)
RAAF 11 Sq.
Executed 3-5-44 by 6th Field Kempei Tai at Talili.

Murphy, John Joseph  Capt.  (Australian)
Aust. Army Coastwatcher
Survived.

Nason, Joseph Gates  Ens.  (American)
USN VF-38
Survived.

Newman, -  1/Lt.  (American)
USAAF
Last seen alive 11-43, fate unknown.

Norman, A.L.  F/O  (Australian)
RAAF
Executed, date unknown.

O'Hagan, -  2/Lt.  (American)
Last seen alive 11-43 in Navy custody, fate unknown.

O'Loughlin, R.B.  F/O  (Australian)
RAAF
Executed, date unknown.

Olley, Fred  Sgt.  (Australian)
RAAF  11 Sq.
Executed 3-5-44 by 6th Field Kempei Tai at Talili.

Osborne, John  Ens.  (American)
USN
Aviator; Major Saiji Matsuda told 1/Lt. James McMurria that Osborne was sent to Japan and arrived safely. Fate unknown.

Palmer, Escoe E.  Sgt.  (American)
USAAF 31BS, 5BG
Survived.

Parker, W.M.  LAC  (Australian)
RAAF
Executed, date unknown.

Peace, -  (American)
USAAF
Executed 10-42.

Phillis, Philip K.  (American)
USN
Executed probably in 1944.

Pockney, Frank Ronald  Lt.  (Australian)
RAAF  11 Sq.
Executed 3-5-44 by 6th Field Kempei Tai at Talili.

Quinones, Alphones D.  1/Lt.  (American)
USAAF 39FS, 35FG
Survived, retired from USAF 1971.

Ramsey, -  Maj.  (British)
Fate unknown.

Ryder, John S.  (American)
USN VP-52
Executed, date unknown.

Sherman, Robert William  1/Lt.  (American)
USMC VMTB-233
Died 6-28-44 of beriberi.

Stacy, Brian  (New Zealander)
RAAF?
Transported to Japan 2-44, fate unknown.

Stewart, Lawson  Sgt.  (American)
USAAF 5BG
Executed 3-5-44 by 6th Field Kempei Tai at Talili.

Stookey, Donald L.  1/Lt..  (American)
USAAF  500BS, 345BG
Executed 3-5-44 by 6th Field Kempei Tai at Talili.

Sugden, Olston Fred  1/Lt.  (American)
USAAF 321BS, 90BG
Executed 3-5-44 by 6th Field Kempei Tai at Talili.

Taylor, Charles  Lt.  (American)
USAAF 80FS
Transported to Japan 2-44, survived.

Teall, Arthur  1/Lt.  (American)
USN VB-12
Taken from Kempei Tai custody by Navy 12-43, fate unknown.

Thomas, Gordon Donald  Sgt.  (Australian)
RAAF  22BS
Executed 3-5-44 by 6th Field Kempei Tai at Talili.

Todd, John Evelyn  Maj.  (Australian)
RAAF  11 Sq.
Died 7-22-44 of dyspepsia.

Tuck, Harold R.  2/Lt.  (American)
USMC VMSB-341
Died 11-12-44 of malaria.

Unruh, Marion Daniel  Col.  (American)
USAAF 5BG
Transported to Japan 2-44, survived.

Vickers, Norman N.  F/Sgt.  (New Zealander)
RNZAF 12 Sq.
Died 7-22-44 of dyspepsia.

Vincent, G.H.  F/Lt.  (Australian)
RAAF
Executed, date unknown.

Walsh, -  (Australian)
RAAF
Executed 1942.

Warren, Charles  F/O  (New Zealander)
RNZAF 20 Sq.
Survived.

Warren, James Arthur  Ens.  (American)
USN VF-33
Captured Kabanga Bay 12-23-43; died 6-3-44 of nephritis.

Wasilevsky, Vincent  Sgt.  (American)
USSAF 23BS
Executed 3-5-44 by 6th Field Kempei Tai at Talili.

Wein, Colin E.  F/Sgt.  (Australian)
RAAF
Executed 3-5-44 by 6th Field Kempei Tai at Talili.

Wells, William Thomson  Ens.  (American)
USN VB-12
Transferred from Kempei Tai custody to Navy 12-19-43, fate unknown.

Weston, -  Capt.  (American)
USAAF
Fate unknown.

Wharton, Sidney F. Jr.  Maj.  (American)
USAAF, 6th Night Fighter Squadron
Fate unknown.

Wisener, Jack King  1/Lt.  (American)
USAAF 65BS, 43BG
Transported to Japan 11-43, survived.

Woodroffe, Roy  (Australian)
RAN
Executed 9-42 by 81st Guards Unit.

Woolley, Frederick  (Australian)
RAAF
Executed 3-5-44 by 6th Field Kempei Tai at Talili.

Wyne, Frank O.  Sgt.  (American)
USAAF 33BS, 90BG
Transported to Japan 11-43, survived.

Zanger, Moszek  1/Lt.  (American)
USMC VMF-222
Captured 12-44, shot to death 7-45 while trying to escape at Tobera.


Note: This is a listing of military prisoners. Many civilians were also held, planters, missionaries, etc. but are not shown here. There were many more prisoners whose unidentified remains were recovered after the war by the Imperial War Graves Commission, Anzac Agency. This is the most complete listing of POWs held at Rabaul, but there are errors in the spelling of surnames because they were transcribed incorrectly more than 50 years ago. Much of the research was by the late Jose L. Holguin of Los Angeles, CA, a former POW at Rabaul and kindly provided to this author by his wife Rebecca.